DISCOVER
MEDITATION

DISCOVER MEDITATION

DORIEL HALL

KATHERINE ARMITAGE
Illustrator

Ulysses Press  Berkeley, CA

1997

Copyright © 1997 Doriel Hall. All rights reserved under International and Pan-American Copyright Conventions, including the right to reproduce this book or portions thereof in any form whatsoever, except for use by a reviewer in connection with a review.

Published by: Ulysses Press
P.O. Box 3440
Berkeley, CA 94703-3440

Library of Congress Catalog Card Number: 97-60157

ISBN: 1-56975-113-7

Printed in the USA by the George Banta Company

10 9 8 7 6 5 4 3 2 1

Editorial and production: Leslie Henriques, Claire Chun, Lily Chou, Nicole O'Hay
Typesetter: David Wells
Cover Design: B & L Design
Indexer: Sayre Van Young

Distributed in the United States by Publishers Group West and in Canada by Raincoast Books

*Dedicated to Paramahansa Satyanda and all who give
unstintingly of their wisdom and love*

TABLE OF CONTENTS

PART ONE

—

WHAT IS MEDITATION?

UNDERSTANDING MEDITATION

The word meditation can be used in two ways. There are techniques of meditation, and there is the state of meditation.

TECHNIQUES OF MEDITATION

When we say that someone is meditating, we usually mean that he or she is engaged in doing one of the techniques of meditation. Some of these techniques are physical, such as sitting cross-legged with your eyes closed. Others are mental, such as visualizing scenes or objects. Whether physical or mental, all the techniques of meditation involve doing something.

The point of this activity is to achieve the state of meditation, which is a way of being rather than doing. It brings healing, clarity and peace where confusion and anxiety existed before. It helps us to cope with the challenges in our lives. Being committed and regular in our practice of the techniques brings many benefits, as long as we focus on what we are doing and not on what we hope to achieve.

THE STATE OF MEDITATION

Through the practice of meditation, we gradually arrive at a stage where much of our time is spent in the state of meditation, even when we are busy. Body and mind can be fully occupied, yet we can still be aware of an inner stillness and peace that spreads through all our activities and touches the people around us.

We have all met the kind of person who never seems rushed and always has time to listen, yet, far from being idle, such people are usually the busiest and most productive, the most loving and supportive, of all those whom we know.

This inner state of meditation is not easy to describe. Perhaps an analogy and a little imagination will help us to appreciate the vast changes in perception that it brings.

LOOKING THROUGH OTHER EYES

Human beings have eyes that are placed at the front of the head and look forward. Both eyes work together to see objects in the round, and to give a sense of distance.

Imagine not having human eyesight, but having to look through the eyes of a fish! You have an eye on each side of your head. The view that you see through each eye is completely different — therefore your world is permanently split in two. The angle of vision of each of your eyes is not very large, so you have to make do with seeing only two small slices of reality. Your world appears to you as unconnected slices of color and movement. You can move your head to change the viewpoint from either eye. Even so, most of your world remains forever out of sight.

Everything appears flat, with two dimensional shapes moving around. Are they friend or foe? As they disappear out of sight of your left eye, will they reappear in front of your right eye? If not, where have they gone? Are they about to attack you from the unknown darkness in front of you?

How does it feel to see the world as a fish does, with double and unconnected vision? You have no wraparound vision to connect your left and right sides with what is in front of you. You have no depth of vision. You cannot see things in the round, nor judge accurately their distance from you — such concepts are inconceivable to you.

"WHEN THINE EYE IS SINGLE . . ."

Now imagine that you have been shown some exercises designed to bring your eyes around to the front of your head. Every day you practice these exercises, prescribed for you by a wise old fish. You cannot foresee what the results will be, because they are outside your present experience. There is no point in speculating. When you ask questions about the purpose of the exercises, you are told: "Just practice them daily and then you will find out," which seems a very unsatisfactory answer.

Then one day something happens. You get a glimpse of the same thing seen from two different angles at once. This is impossible! Right and left have always been on opposite sides before, separated by a huge barrier of darkness.

The next revelation is that of depth. You manage to get the two images of the same object lined up and properly focused. The two become one, and this one looks totally different from anything you have ever seen before. It is no longer flat, yet you have no words to express roundness. You cannot talk about distance either, although you are experiencing it.

You start trying to explain to another fish how your perception of the world around you has changed, but you are not believed. You may even be considered mad and dangerous to know. In the end, you just say: "Keep doing the exercises and you will find out for yourself."

Jesus said: "When thine eye is single thy whole body also is full of light."[1] In the East this is called enlightenment, and is traditionally achieved through the practice of meditation techniques.

These techniques have been successfully practiced by millions of ordinary people all over the world for thousands of years. It has not even been necessary to understand how or why they work. Most people in the past, being uneducated, did not even ask, instead trusting their teachers to lead them. The teachers underwent rigorous training in their particular tradition, which was usually embedded in their religion. In this way, the traditional techniques have been preserved for our use today. They have also been hidden behind alien and colorful rituals that may not appeal to our modern Western minds.

Discover Meditation aims to present the techniques of meditation in the simplest possible way, stripped of the confusing language that time and tradition has laid upon them. The techniques work, and are not difficult to do or to understand. The only thing you need to begin with — and to go on with — is commitment to regular practice.

[1] Luke 11:34, *The Bible*, Authorized Version.

THE ORIGINS OF
MEDITATION

SEEING IN A NEW WAY

The state of meditation is the state of seeing with the mind's eye in a new way. Things come together and fall into place. What seemed like irreconcilable opposites become complementary to each other and merge, while still retaining their essential differences. This bringing together is a creative act, from which entirely new insights arise.

The state of meditation allows a wider, more comprehensive view of things. It is progressive, with each new stage coming as a wonderful revelation. It is a journey without end, bringing healing and integration along the way. It is our evolutionary path, which we can help to speed up if we are prepared to make the effort.

MEDITATION HAS ALWAYS BEEN WITH US

Meditation techniques have always been part of the attempt to alter the natural human condition, with its physical pains, its changeable and unstable emotions, and its self-centered and deluded thinking.

The civilized ideal has always been to lift human consciousness to an abiding state of peace, wholeness and universal love. The methods that have evolved to achieve this aim are many and varied. Most of them include self-discipline, self-knowledge and self-surrender — so that body, mind and emotions are all involved.

Five thousand years ago, the civilization of Ancient Egypt was using these very methods. The Great Pyramid was built about this time, and it is clear from the hieroglyphs that meditation formed an important part of priestly life. Ceramic statues, also made about 5,000 years ago, were discovered intact during excavations of the Dravidian civilization at Mohenjo Daro in the Indus basin. They depict Yogis in meditation.

Four thousand years ago the book called the *I Ching* was being created in China, and we still benefit from its insights today. The great prophets of the Old Testament lived 3,500 years ago. The sacred books called the *Vedas* were being written around this time in India, and these still form the basis of Hindu religious thought. All these insights arose in higher states of consciousness during meditation, and were first uttered by sages, saints or seers who became spiritual giants as a result of lives shaped by meditation.

MEDITATION IS A NATURAL STATE

At the same time, it seems that the state of meditation is a natural state, which can sometimes arise spontaneously. Meditation is a state of relaxed alertness, a responsive state, unclouded by physical discomfort, self-centered emotions or personal opinions. A wider view becomes possible, as heart and mind expand beyond the confines of the personal self.

WATCHING OURSELVES

Meditation is a state of mind, a point of view about the world and ourselves. It does not radiate outward from our own ego center, but is diffused across the scene that we find ourselves in. It is as though we were sitting comfortably in an auditorium and watching ourselves taking part in a play on the stage. We observe ourselves and our lives from outside the world we are living in — we are uninvolved witnesses of what is going on in that world. At the same time we remain involved in the parts we are playing, agonizing over our moment-to-moment decisions and actions. Our world is both real and not real, when we are in the meditative state.

"ALL THE WORLD'S A STAGE . . . "

Shakespeare said: "All the world's a stage and all the men and women merely players . . . "[1] This idea is very ancient, appearing in both Eastern and Western religious traditions. In the East, life is seen as a game played by consciousness for its own amusement. In the West, we are told that God is working his purpose out as year succeeds to year. The Ancient Greeks and Romans portrayed their gods as playing games with mere mortals — who were usually the losers!

This idea is also very modern, tying in with the theory of evolution, which can be seen as a process. Increasingly complex structures evolve, becoming ever more conscious as they do so. It now seems as if consciousness, rather than directing the natural world from outside it, is actually evolving from within it.

Theorizing about consciousness will not make us more conscious — this is the aim of meditation, which bypasses thought altogether. As a result of time spent in meditation, we return to our thinking processes with a clear and rested mind. We practice meditation to help us to see more clearly and to become more aware. We can increase our awareness of our own selves, of how we "tick" and of what (or who) "pushes our buttons." And we can open up to more of the ongoing "story" that we find ourselves in, and to those around us who are also involved in it.

HUMAN PUPPETS ON THE STAGE OF LIFE

Let us imagine a puppet theatre. The puppets seem to move independently, but we know that they are marionettes. They are attached to wires that are operated by an unseen hand. The owner of this hand has to follow the instructions of a director, otherwise there would be mayhem on stage. The director, in turn, is following a script written by someone else.

Even the author is not totally free. He or she is limited by the capacities of the puppets and the understanding of the audience. Every action on every stage is part of a stream of communication that flows between a particular author and a particular audience. All the intervening levels — the stage, the puppets, the wires, the puppeteers and the director — merely serve as channels for this continuous process of communication.

Meditation is the regular discipline of watching and listening to communication itself, and of becoming an open and willing channel through which it can flow.

Puppets are a good analogy for human beings, because the lines of communication are more obvious than they are in real life. The puppet itself (the body) can only move when the puppeteer (the mind) tells it to. The puppeteer holds a frame (the brain), where all the wires attached to the puppet come together. These wires are the nervous system, by which the brain communicates with the body.

The puppeteer, who is holding the frame in his hand, obeys a director, who represents all our cultural and ethical programming, and our conditioned responses to life. This director can be both demanding and limiting — often far more than we realize. Suppose the author plans to introduce a completely new style or concept into the story — evolution is supposed to be progressive, after all! The director, however, feels safer with tradition, and will do everything possible to resist change. This is why it is so difficult to break old habits and to establish new ones.

The author has many names, such as Higher Self, Universal Self, Supreme Consciousness, God, Love. How can we, as puppets on the stage of life, express more fully the intentions of the author? The practice of meditation provides a way that has been used all over the world for thousands of years and also inspires much of the innovative thinking that is now appearing in the West.

[1] William Shakespeare, *As You Like It*, Act 2.

HEALING WITH
MEDITATION

A FRESH START

Meditation wipes the slate clean of old conditioning and habits, so that new insights can arise to
lead us forward in our personal evolution. We in
turn affect all who are involved with us.

The practice of meditation leads to the settled
mind which rests in itself, passively observing or
listening to the flow of communication passing
through it. There is neither rejection nor clinging
— all is accepted, savored and allowed to pass on
its way. This results in more responsive attitudes
to others, and in the healing of old hurts.

There is also a universal level of meditation that
lies beyond personal concerns, and sometimes
connects us to a collective pool of consciousness.
In this way, we may gain access to fresh insights,
which inspire new — or half-forgotten — ways of
looking at the world.

This fresh start is worth all the time, effort and discipline we put into our meditation practice. The wisdom distilled from our life's experiences remains with us, but we now see with new eyes. Our view is stripped of the layers of conditioning that have been building up ever since our birth. This freedom from programming allows us to relate differently to the circumstances and people in our lives. It is then up to us to bring about positive changes in our attitudes and behavior.

The regular practice of meditation carries over into our daily lives, so that we can "count to ten" instead of reacting with our usual, programmed response to a situation. Such pauses in our normal pattern give us time to see ourselves behaving like puppets, and letting our "wires" be jerked without our conscious consent.

CONSCIOUS LISTENING

The world "speaks" to us continuously through our sensory perceptions — our five senses — and we relay this information to the brain via the nervous system. The brain works like a computer: it processes the information it receives according to how it has been programmed by our previous experience and training. Often the thinking mind is not involved, and our reactions are unconscious, as when we drive a car.

Meditation helps us to become more conscious of our own bodies and to listen, with respect, to what they are telling us. This helps us to recognize — and then minimize — whatever is causing physical disharmony and stress — an important aspect of healing. Communication is always a two-way process — there must be at least one who "speaks" and one who "listens." Meditation can be described as conscious listening.

It is so much more constructive to attend to the input coming from the world, from other people and from within ourselves, than it is to drown this communication by a mental sea of words. Unfortunately, our minds seldom stop talking long enough for us to attend to anything except our own mental dialogue — this carries on even while we are conversing with others.

The practice of meditation teaches us to listen and to look, and to accept what is there without censorship. Acceptance is an important part of healing. However much we may regret certain qualities that we find in ourselves or others, anger or denial can only make things worse.

RESTORING WHOLENESS WITHIN OURSELVES

The practice of meditation brings us to a state of harmony, of equilibrium, within our bodies, energies and mind. Such a state by its very nature transcends all imbalances and disharmony. It is a state of wholeness.

Healing can be described as the restoration of wholeness. Sometimes this process brings about a cure for symptoms of disharmony that may cause physical pain, emotional distress, or mental blockages. It cannot always do so, however, as some diseases are irreversible, some conditions are present from birth and cannot be changed, and some accidents cause permanent damage.

Meditation is not a panacea for every ill that may befall us. What it can do is to help us to sort out what can, and what cannot, be changed. There is a famous prayer, attributed to St. Richard of Chichester: "Give us the fortitude to accept the things we cannot change, the courage to change the things we can, and the wisdom to know the difference."[1] Fortitude, courage and wisdom are enhanced by the practice of meditation, which gives us a firm base from which to accept things as they are.

Even prayer — or perhaps especially prayer — starts from this base. We are as we are — imperfect. To accept ourselves without pretense is the start of a willingness to change. From there follows the request for divine help, and a quiet readiness to hear the answers we are given.

SELF-PROTECTING SCREENS

If we are trying to pretend that we are something other than we suspect ourselves to be, and are being very careful not to look at ourselves too closely, we cannot help blocking communication with others. We erect walls that obstruct the flow both in and our of our ego castle.

First we need to take a long, detached look at ourselves, and then come to terms with the shortfall between what we would like to be and what we actually are. These preliminary tasks can be done most easily when we have already achieved a state of harmony and are strong enough to take the shock! This strength is built up gradually by periods of regular meditation.

Self-acceptance, without flinching, is the start of emotional healing. A sense of humor is also a great help — to be able to laugh affectionately at our own foibles takes the sting out of self-discovery. Once energy begins to flow around our self-protecting screens and walls, they will begin to tumble.

Acceptance of ourselves leads automatically to two things:

- to communication with other imperfect beings

- to communication with the perfect self, of which we all form tiny parts

If we can see ourselves as limited, imperfect fragments of a limitless and perfect whole — and other beings as wonderfully diverse fragments of the same whole — our world view will change dramatically. We can then let go of the fear and competitiveness of "it's either them or me," and welcome the warmth and togetherness of "you and me within the whole."

How Long Will it Take?

Some traditions say that it can take thousands of lifetimes, but that it is also achievable in this life. Others suggest a long period of learning, or "purgatory," rather than actual physical lives. Some believe that we can evolve by our own efforts, others that we must rely on divine help, yet others that a marriage of the two is essential.

All forward-looking thinkers agree that the goal of humanity should be to evolve from our present "either/or" view of life into greater communication and love. In the late twentieth century we are all global neighbors, so it is vital that we get started on our personal evolution, before we destroy our world.

Non-Attachment

Meditation teaches us how to really listen, without jumping in and getting involved in a conversation. This skill can then be used to hear what our bodies, the world and the people around us are trying to tell us. We may not feel flattered by what we hear, but at least we are engaging in real communication.

The listening of meditation is non-attached — receptive to all input, reserving judgment on what is heard until it can be properly assessed. Like counting to ten, the interval between receiving information and reacting to it, or judging it in relation to our own interests and self esteem, gets longer the more we practice meditation. We come to see that it is seldom helpful or appropriate to react immediately, off-loading our anger or instant advice.

In any genuinely threatening situation we do need to react swiftly and to make instant judgments, however. Unfortunately, we are apt to assume that we are being threatened when we are not. We leap into defensive mode automatically, becoming needlessly frightened or angry, which in turn sparks off fear and anger in those around us, setting up a vicious circle of tension and mistrust.

The practice of meditation makes us more easy going, more peaceable and easier to live with. Before long, we feel kinder vibrations coming back to us. All communication is like a boomerang: we get back what we send out.

Survival Depends upon Being Heard

We were born expecting the world to satisfy all our needs — and for most of us it doesn't. Up to eighty per cent of modern Western families are said to be dysfunctional, which means that no one in such a family gets what they truly need.

A human child cannot survive on its own, so it is programmed to expect that adults will listen and respond to its cries for help. Adults, however, may sometimes have forgotten how to listen, and may be too wrapped up in their own concerns to hear the child's distress. Such a child grows up to perceive the world as a harsh, uncaring place.

Our most primitive and basic concern is for our own survival, safety and well-being. We are programmed to look after Number One. This is the basis of all evolution, including human evolution. If any of our five senses report back to us that we have something to fear from the outside world, we will react instinctively, without thinking.

Yet how often do we really have anything to fear? There is an old taunt: "Sticks and stones may break my bones, but words can never hurt me." So why do we fear what people think or say about us?

Fear Is Always Physical

Fear is always physical — we feel fear in our bodies, and we are fearful for our bodies. We fear pain, injury and death. In common with many mammalian species, we are completely helpless at birth. Without the care of our parents, or substitute caring from other adults, we could not survive. Therefore we depend totally upon their attention and goodwill.

Needless to say, it is impossible that we should always have these ministrations, so we quickly learn to fear their absence, lack of attention, anger, etc. This fear of abandonment is carried with us through life — or until we learn to feel secure without having to rely totally upon other, more supposedly grown-up people.

Because fear is felt in the body, chronic and unrecognized anxiety can cause physical illness. The recognition and removal of the fear of being abandoned is one of the tasks of modern psychotherapy, often accompanied by regular meditation. This, in turn, can bring physical as well as emotional and mental healing.

Fear can become a habit that is hard to break, even when we know that we are in no danger of immediate extinction. Much of our adult behavior may still be based upon the attempt to be noticed favorably by those who wield power over us. Our worst nightmare is to be ignored or abandoned. This pattern is programmed into the brain's computer, and will remain there. It can even be passed on to future generations along with all our other negative conditioning, until a conscious effort is made to change it.

Meditation can help in many ways. It teaches us how to stop and listen, and to accept that what is, is. Once we can look at things as they truly are, it becomes possible to change our attitudes to the people and circumstances in our lives. We can get in touch with higher aspects of ourselves, and draw support and guidance from within. We can become conscious channels for the type of communication that we all long for — a non-judgmental, two-way traffic of love.

LOVE HEALS

It is love that heals, rather than any techniques. We use the techniques to help us to get to know and accept ourselves. To know all is to understand all. To understand all is to accept all. To accept all is to forgive all. To forgive all is to love all. Or as Madame de Staël put it: "To know all makes one tolerant."[2] This is how attitudes are changed — toward ourselves, then our friends, then our enemies, then all the world. A very famous meditation technique is to visualize love radiating outward from our hearts toward all sentient beings.

Love can only express itself through communication, even if all that is possible is a loving attitude that seems totally one-sided. We can develop this unilateral attitude — perhaps it would be more accurate to say that we can uncover it, as we let go of layers of conditioning and shells of self-protection. We can rediscover the world as it once seemed, before we felt lonely and afraid.

NATURE IS ONE

The universe is once again coming to be recognized in the West — as it always has been in the East — as an indivisible and interdependent whole.

We are living in a wonderful age, where traditions and ideas that were for centuries seen as mutually exclusive are now coming together as different facets of the same reality. Eminent physicists of the modern age have led the way. Albert Einstein came to realize that matter and energy are different aspects of the same "stuff," and expressed this in his famous equation $e = mc^2$ (energy = matter × the speed of light squared).

Sir James Jeans added mind to matter and energy in his famous quotation: "The universe looks less and less like a great machine and more and more like a great thought."[3] Sir

Arthur Eddington went even further: "The stuff of the world is mind stuff."[4]

Healing with meditation deals with this "mind stuff," bringing body, energy and mind into harmony with each other by changing what the mind's eye perceives. Most of the time our world appears to us as fragmented. Things seem separate and solid. We cannot see energies such as electricity or gravity, water or wind power, we can only become aware of their effects upon solid objects. Mind, or intelligence, is even more mysterious. We know, but seldom experience for ourselves, that matter, energy and mind must all be present in every living thing.

If we leave no space in our lives to "sit and stare" we may become overwhelmingly depressed and weighed down by feelings of separation and isolation. We need to reconnect, to take time out to appreciate the interlocking wholeness of nature. Once in a state of meditation, we get a feeling of awe and wonder. Doing nothing, thinking nothing, relaxed yet wide awake, we suddenly become part of the majestic wholeness.

MEDITATION WORKS

Meditation does work. Millions of learned and loving people have practiced it throughout the ages, because it clears the mind and opens the heart. Highly educated priests and sages spent their lives pursuing and teaching the way to enlightenment. The techniques have been incorporated into the world's great philosophies and religions, and have been used by millions of people through the ages.

The current interest in meditation has inspired many modern teachers to simplify the ancient techniques, and to strip them of the cultural accretions of centuries. In this way, meditation has become accessible to people who may not wish to get involved in a religious tradition, but who do wish to change themselves and to improve the quality of their lives and relationships.

Part Two sets out to explain meditation techniques in straightforward, easy-to-follow terms.

[1] Displayed in Chichester Cathedral, Sussex, England.

[2] Madame de Stael, Corinne, France 1807.

[3] Quoted by Kit Pedlar, *Mind Over Matter*, London: Granada 1981, p. 36.

[4] Ibid.

PART TWO

HOW TO MEDITATE

SETTING THE SCENE

THE RIGHT CONDITIONS

The state of meditation can sometimes occur spontaneously, when all the conditions are just right. However, most of us need to work quite hard at our meditation techniques in order to get into the right frame of mind.

There are five basic requirements:

- the body must be comfortable and still
- the internal energies need to be in balance
- the mind must remain focused and not be allowed to wander
- the heart must be at peace
- you must wait patiently, without expectations

You first need to learn how to sit comfortably in a suitable position, and to practice this position until you can remain in it, relaxed yet alert, for half an hour or more.

You may need to practice breathing exercises to bring the internal energies into a state of harmony. Otherwise you will be hampered in your practice by restlessness of one sort or another — traditionally known as distractions.

You should focus your mind on one thing only, which can be an external or internal object. You should become aware of when your mind wanders — as it will — and gently bring it back into focus.

Your heart should become naturally peaceful and serene as a result of attending to your body, breathing and mind. If it remains disturbed or unhappy, there are many techniques to help you to gain inner tranquillity when negative emotions beset you.

Having got yourself ready for the state of meditation to arise in you, *do nothing*. Maintain your stillness and wait tranquilly — simply grateful for the opportunity to receive. You are like a radio receiver tuned in to catch whatever may come to you from beyond.

WHERE, WHEN AND HOW OFTEN SHOULD YOU MEDITATE?

The first consideration is where to practice. Clearly you need somewhere quiet, where you can be sure you will not be interrupted — especially by the telephone. A special room would be ideal, with a notice on the door saying "Do not disturb." In some families, however, such a notice would be an invitation to teasing and constant interruption. Whatever place you designate, it should be comfortably warm, ventilated and free from drafts.

Meditation practice involves sitting still, which causes the body temperature to drop, so you will need a light shawl or blanket to keep you warm. You will also need firm cushions to sit on, or a suitable stool or chair. Some people like to use flowers or incense, and perhaps music. You may want to keep special pictures or objects in your meditation space.

If you have to recreate this space from day to day, or to set it up wherever happens to be most convenient, then it is helpful to keep a special rug to delineate your meditation space. As you unroll it and set up your cushions, the atmosphere quickly changes — almost as though the heightened vibrations were preserved in the rug itself and unfolded into the air as you spread it out on the floor.

WHEN TO PRACTICE

The second consideration is time. When, in a normal day, can you expect to have half an hour or so to yourself? The meditation methods you choose will be influenced by how many people make demands upon your time, and by how long you can be alone during each day. Of course it is possible and valuable to meditate in a group — but this is usually in addition to private practice, and not as a substitute for it.

The traditional times for meditation are dawn and dusk. Some deeper reasons for this are explained later in the book, but there are also very practical reasons. In countries closer to the Equator, the seasons are not as variable as they are further north or south, so the rhythms of light and darkness provide a good framework for daily life. In rural communities life is also lived by the passage of the sun and, in the days before electric light, it made sense for everyone to rise at dawn and to settle down for the night soon after dusk.

Despite time-changes and artificial daylight, it is still a good idea to practice meditation before you start your day and before you finish it. Can you meditate in bed? Some would say that they can not. But if you sleep alone, where else is as warm, private and filled with your personal vibrations as your own bed? There is one important proviso, however: to meditate you must be both relaxed *and* wide awake.

In the morning you will probably need to set your alarm, allowing yourself time to wake up properly, wash, make a hot drink, sit bolt upright in bed with a shawl around you, and prepare your mind for meditation. Otherwise you will simply daydream — relaxed but not alert — and the precious time will be wasted.

The same considerations apply to meditation in bed before going to sleep. You can sit up and review the day in your mind, accepting all that has occurred to you and all that you have said or done. Then let it all go, and do your meditation practice. Or you can read a few lines of an inspirational text, and let the meaning sink in without trying to "get your mind around it." Then do your meditation practice.

Most times of the day are suitable for meditation practice, as long as you can be in a relaxed but alert state. This is difficult after meals, though, or when you are upset or rushed.

How Often to Meditate

The third consideration — which may affect both place and time — is regularity, the building up of a firm habit. Once established, the habit of meditation becomes an important part of your life. So choose a place and time that you can stick to and practice in every day — unless something really exceptional prevents you.

There will inevitably be times when you have to miss a session, but carry on (especially at the beginning) working to establish regularity. It is worth the effort to overcome the strong habit of *not* practicing meditation. Most of us are quite happy to experiment with something new, and to do it when we feel like it. We are, however, usually resistant to changing our life-long habits, and so you will need determination to overcome this natural resistance.

5

DECIDING HOW TO SIT

——

Can you sit cross-legged on the floor? Could you ever — perhaps when you were younger? Since this is a very good position for meditation, it is well worth practicing sitting in this position, if you can. If you know it would never be possible for you, then there are good alternatives — such as sitting in a chair. You can start with the simplest possible position suitable for meditation practice, and work up to the more demanding positions.

It is essential that the spine should be vertical, so no leaning back posture is appropriate. Soft armchairs are not suitable, but a hard armchair may be — if you can arrange cushions behind you to keep yourself sitting bolt upright. A hard, upright chair is good, but you will need to sit firmly on it with your spine erect and vertical, your thighs at right angles to your spine and your shins also vertical. If your feet do not rest flat upon the floor in this position, you will need to place them on a book, block or cushion so that you are firmly "grounded."

A hard chair with arms may be comfortable, but only if the arms are at the right height for you. Your shoulders need to be relaxed, but chair arms that are too high for you will push your shoulders up and make you ache. Chair arms that are too low will make you lean either forward or back to rest your forearms. It is well worth experimenting to get yourself comfortable *and* upright. Sit "tall," as described below.

THE EGYPTIAN POSITION

Sitting bolt upright on a hard chair is called the Egyptian position, because it appears so often in Egyptian hieroglyphics. You can rest your hands in your lap, palms up, with one hand resting upon the other — this is sometimes called the gesture of peace, especially when the tips of the thumbs are touching. The Buddha is often shown with his hands in his lap in this position. It is very relaxing and soothing, conveying a feeling that your energies are being contained. If you are using a chair with arms, you can rest one hand on each arm, with the palms down and the forearms comfortably supported.

It is not easy to sit bolt upright in bed unless you can bend your knees out to the sides, no matter how many pillows you use. Some adaptation of a cross-legged position is best.

THE BUDDHIST POSITION

The next easiest position is probably the one that Buddhists adopt. Buddhist monasteries often provide special cushions for meditation practice. These are round and very firm, about six inches high and a foot or so across. You kneel up with your knees apart, push the cushion underneath you and sit astride it. Your knees and shins rest on the floor each

The Egyptian position

side of the cushion, with your feet relaxed and pointing out behind you. You can use a couple of blankets rolled into a firm sausage, perhaps with a cushion on top, to take the place of the special meditation cushion. Make sure you are sitting high enough to be comfortable.

As you lower yourself down from the kneeling position, it is important to tuck the coccyx (tailbone) under, to lengthen and straighten the lower back as you sit down. The aim is to

The Buddhist position

draw the spine upward, lengthening it. Next, you pull the navel back toward the spine, and stretch up from the waist. Then you lift the sternum (breast bone), which is like a hinge that is moveable above the waist and fixed at the collarbones. As you lift the bottom end of this "hinge," you create space between the chest and the abdomen. So often we slump in this area when we feel tired or dispirited, and this just makes us feel worse. Finally, the head should pull up from the top of the spine, with the chin level and not poking either forward or upward. The shoulders and arms should remain relaxed, with the hands folded in the lap, palms up as described above.

The Buddhist position is one of great poise. Notice how a dancer adjusts the body — tail under, waist back, chest up, head erect, chin level. This positive stance can be adopted whenever you are sitting, standing or walking, and you will feel very much better for it. The spine rises up confidently, allowing plenty of space for the internal organs to do their work, whereas a slumped position crowds them and constricts the flow of blood traveling around the body.

If you prefer, the hands can rest on the knees or thighs, palms down. You may like to join the tips of the thumbs and forefingers together in the gesture of wisdom, keeping the other three fingers loosely together and the palms down. Another version is to tuck the fingernail of the forefinger under the fleshy pad of the thumb. Experiment until you find the best hand position for you.

Meditation stools are also available. These are usually made of wood, with the seat sloping forward and raised about nine inches from the floor. To sit on one, you kneel up in front of it, with your shins on the floor underneath the stool and your feet pointing out behind. Then lower yourself down onto it, keeping the back straight as described above.

As you can see, the whole body is involved in the practice of meditation — and you should remain aware of every part of it until you deliberately focus your attention elsewhere for the next part of the process.

KNEELING

A Yoga position that can be used is simply to sit down on your heels from a kneeling position. The trouble with this is that it compresses the lower abdomen somewhat. To avoid this, you can place a cushion on your calves, thus raising the buttocks a little. Keeping the knees apart may also help. You need to feel that your internal energies can move freely through the body, with no part "closed" or "sealed off."

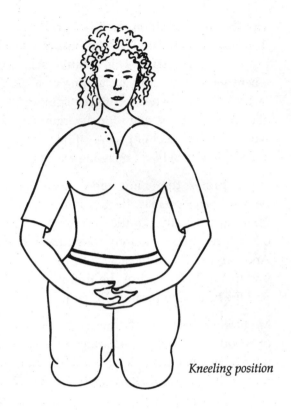

Kneeling position

THE POSITION OF THE ADEPT

The Yoga position of the adept is excellent. It may take a while to loosen up and remain comfortable in it, but it is well worth the effort to do so. Start by sitting on one or two firm cushions — or a cushion on top of a folded blanket — with your legs spread out as wide as possible in front of you. Keep your knees straight and relaxed on the floor, with your toes turned up and pointing to the ceiling.

To ease out the hip joints, lean forward — keeping your legs and feet in position — and "walk" your fingers forward an inch at a time. When you have reached your limit, stay there for a few moments, then "walk" your fingers back again. Repeat this a few times on each occasion, and do this exer-

Position of the adept

cise frequently. If your hips are very stiff or painful to begin with, or if you are arthritic, it is probably best not to persevere with this exercise and to choose another sitting position instead. Ordinary stiffness from lack of use of the relevant muscles, however, will soon wear off with practice and you will begin to feel much looser.

The next stage is to bend one knee, and keeping the thigh and knee in position on the floor, slide your foot along the floor until the heel comes against your body, with the sole pushed against the opposite groin and thigh. The bent knee must stay on the floor — if it lifts, you need to sit on more cushions. It is essential that you maintain the support of the knee against the floor, and later on, both knees against the floor, to take the weight off your lower back.

You can do all sorts of meditation exercises in this position, which will soon become very comfortable, though do be sure to change legs from time to time. You will feel well balanced and secure as you sit with your spine erect and your hands in your lap in the gesture of peace, or on your thighs in the ges-

ture of wisdom. If you want to, you can let your hands roll over so that the palms face upward in a receptive position.

When you feel ready, bend the second knee and slide the second foot along the floor to press against the first, both heels up and in line, both knees on the floor. This is a very stable position, suitable for entering states of deep meditation when you have forgotten all about your body.

This position is also excellent for sitting up in bed, which is a great bonus, especially in cold weather, because it is important to avoid becoming chilly while practicing meditation. You may like to put a pillow behind you or underneath you. A hard mattress is best, as a soft one will make you feel unstable.

It is extremely important to sit comfortably, with the spine erect and a firm base for support. It is worth experimenting and then perfecting your chosen position. Sit in it on every

possible occasion — for instance, to read a book or to watch television. It will soon become second nature to you.

6

USING THE BREATH

STRESS AND THE BREATH

All our bodily systems are influenced by the stresses our world places upon us and by our emotional reactions to those stresses. We can feel our breath gasping and our hearts thumping when we get a sudden fright, or our digestions churning painfully after eating too much of the wrong kind of food. These are the natural effects of stress, of one sort or another, and are outside our voluntary control.

Too much stress, over a prolonged period, can upset the bodily systems that have to deal with it each time it occurs. We may end up with a strained heart, or an ulcer in the digestive system. We can try to live our lives in such a way that we avoid all stress — but this is an impossible dream for most of us. In any case, it is likely to be counterproductive in the end. Circumstances change, and we are bound to get into a really stressful situation eventually, which will knock us sideways because we have not learned how to deal with stress.

On the other hand, if we have learned how to limit the effects of stress as it occurs in daily life — rather than trying to escape from it altogether — we will cope far better with major problems when they inevitably arise, and enjoy life more meanwhile.

What has this all this to do with breathing? The answer is that of all the systems of the body, breathing is the only one over which we can gain any degree of conscious control. When we notice that our breathing has changed from its natural flow, and has become stressed, we can *change it back again* and undo the stress.

As the breath returns to its usual pattern, a signal is sent to the brain which says: "All is well, panic over!" And it is, because the brain accepts this message. All the systems of the body come off red alert and return to their natural activities.

One of the most harmful effects of allowing ourselves to remain in a prolonged state of stress is that the systems of the body are kept in a state of imbalance. Some are overactive, others suppressed. The overactive systems eventually suffer from exhaustion, while the suppressed systems are unable to get on with the jobs for which they were designed.

When we are in a state of stress the immune system is suppressed, so infections are more likely to take hold. Ongoing diseases are unchecked, because the "soldiers" of the immune system are prevented from fighting off the enemy. Repair and maintenance of the body's cells is halted. Rest is deferred until the brain takes us off red alert, so we feel more and more tired and depleted. The digestive system is suppressed for the time being — and how long is that? Meanwhile, food can go rotten inside us so that we absorb poisons as well as essential nutrients. We may become constipated, through suppression of the natural movements of the intestines. The list of the harmful effects of prolonged stress on those functions of the body that are being suppressed seems endless!

We are usually more conscious of the undesirable effects of prolonged stress on those functions that are continually overactive — tension in the muscles, causing tiredness and pain, thoughts chasing each other round in our brains so that we cannot concentrate, emotional anxiety causing vague feelings of misery, etc. We seem to be on a treadmill that we cannot get off.

Meditation, however, is all about *stopping* for regular, brief periods, so that we can take an honest, objective look at our condition. We can then start to bring ourselves back into harmony and to re-balance our systems, simply by working with the breath.

EXERCISE ONE
WATCHING THE BREATH

Once you are comfortably seated, the next stage is to close your eyes and start to watch yourself breathing, "looking" and "feeling" from the inside. You need to be careful to observe without allowing your observation to affect your breathing. Some people are so wary of being "looked at" — even by themselves — that self-observation makes them feel anxious and tense. The practice of meditation is meant to expose ourselves to ourselves, however, as only in this way can we see what we want to change and then set about doing so.

So, sitting comfortably in the meditation position you have been practicing, close your eyes and watch yourself breathing for a moment or two. Stop at once if you start to feel ill at ease. Open your eyes and look around. Then attend to the position of your body, stretching up a little more through the spine, relaxing your hands and your face.

When you are ready, start again. Close your eyes and focus on your natural breath, as it flows in and out, in and out. This exercise will soon become easy and very soothing, once your shyness with yourself wears off. You will begin to find that you automatically relax and shed accumulated tensions as soon as you start to focus on your breathing.

The next stage is to consider changing the pattern of your breathing.

EXERCISE TWO
DEEPENING THE BREATH

The upper chest may be moving more than the lower part, causing your breathing to be shallow and rather fast, as though you were permanently anxious or alarmed. This is a very common imbalance, due to "getting stuck" in a stressful reaction to a situation that may even have occurred — and been resolved — many years ago. Your breathing pattern has simply become a habit.

Any imbalance will eventually cause problems, both to the overactive and to the suppressed parts of the system. Overactive upper breathing, being rapid and shallow, also makes the heart beat more quickly. The heartbeat and the breath are closely linked, as we shall see. This kind of breathing is also a panic reaction, telling the brain to keep the red alert button switched on when, in fact, there is nothing to panic about. So it may even make irrational fears more likely to develop. It is present in asthmatics, who find it very hard to breathe slowly and deeply.

With this breathing pattern, the lower part of the chest, and the diaphragm muscle that separates the chest from the abdomen, are both suppressed, which causes many problems. The lower lungs become a wonderful place for germs to breed, because stale air — which is warm and damp — is not being expelled. In addition, the abdominal organs below the diaphragm are not being massaged, because the diaphragm is not pumping up and down as it should. This results in stale blood not being properly removed and replaced by fresh blood, encouraging infection and lack of efficiency in the abdominal area. One small imbalance can affect many areas.

To breathe more fully and deeply, it is essential to sit up straight, as discussed in the last chapter, to allow room for the diaphragm to move freely above the waist. Raise the sternum (the "hinging" breastbone) and *keep it raised*, even as you breathe out. You will then find that you have to use your diaphragm to breathe. This may feel strange at first, but persevere for a few breaths. Then rest, and start again when you are ready. It takes time to change the habits of years — you only need to practice for a few minutes at a time, but do so regularly.

You may find it helpful to place one hand on your breastbone, to check that it stays raised and does not slump down again, and the other hand just above your waist to feel the movement of the diaphragm muscle. It pushes *down* as you breathe *in*, squeezing the organs beneath, and *up* as you breathe *out*, releasing the organs so that fresh blood can flow into them.

Deep breathing — often called the complete breath — is wonderfully revitalizing. You can do it anytime once you know how, as long as your spine is stretched rather than slumped.

EXERCISE THREE
MAKING THE OUTBREATH LONGER

Another very common breathing habit is to fail to allow enough time to breathe out fully. The muscles of the chest and diaphragm need to *relax* to make the chest space smaller — which forces out the excess air (breathing out). If you feel, or have felt, very tense, you may have become unable to relax these muscles fully. Once you are aware of this — through your observation practice — it is not difficult gradually to lengthen the time that it takes to breathe out.

Breathing in is connected with "taking." Anyone who has ever felt deprived is apt thereafter to make doubly sure that they are getting "enough" — he or she may amass things, or simply take in great gulps of air.

Breathing out is connected with "letting go." If you have experienced not getting "enough," it is hard to let go of some of what you already have. Yet you must let go of the stale air in your lungs, because it is of no further use to you — and it is occupying the space that fresh air needs to come into. You cannot breathe *in* fully until you have breathed *out* fully. You need literally to relax your muscles and let go of the stale air in your lungs. For many people — especially asthmatics — the very thought of letting go makes them tighten up and therefore hold the stale air in.

An easy way to learn to let go is to count "one. . . and. . . two . . . and. . . ," etc., as you breathe out. Notice what number you reached. Now count exactly the same number as you breathe in — and then start to breathe out again, counting the *same* number. And so on. To begin with, it may feel easier to shorten the breath in than to lengthen the breath out, but as you begin to relax, you will find that you can add another number as you breathe out — which sets a new pattern for breathing in again. Soon you may add another number. But make haste slowly — if you set up a stressful situation for yourself you will once again find yourself feeling "short of breath."

You will feel wonderfully calm and centered as your breathing in and breathing out become balanced. When you have reached this stage you can go further — make your outward breath (the relaxing, letting go half of the cycle) a little

longer than your inward breath. This is perfectly natural —
often expressed as a long luxurious sigh, as you stretch and
relax, or a big yawn. Singing also forces you to breathe out
very slowly. If you do all these things regularly, you will feel
much more relaxed.

Exercise Four
Balancing Left and Right

There is a theory that the human brain is divided into two
hemispheres that each have their own special functions —
as well as probably sharing other functions. This idea is
quite new to the West, but known to Eastern Yogis for centuries. They have developed a breathing exercise designed
to balance both sides of the brain — and, thereby, all the
"pairs of opposites" that they govern.

The left side of the brain, which governs the right side of the
body, is generally concerned with logical thinking, speech
and practical matters. For many of us, the right hand, foot
and eye are the dominant ones. When we "put our best foot
forward," it is usually the right foot, and our right hand
may be better coordinated than our left. This is probably
cultural — people used to have to conform to the norm,
which was to be right-handed. But why was it accepted as
the dominant side? Was it because logical, practical people
who could express themselves clearly were considered more
useful — and less trouble — to society?

The right side of the brain, which governs the left side of the
body, is concerned with space, creativity and intuition. It
sees things all of a piece rather than sequentially, and is
good at what Edward de Bono has called lateral thinking —
the unexpected sideways jump by which new discoveries
are made. In Latin, left is called *sinister*, or "hidden." Is it
coincidental that it is currently fashionable to let children
grow up left-handed? In these rapidly changing times, society is in great need of people with new ideas.

Yogis consider that the left side of the brain (and right side of the body) is concerned with physical, dynamic things and with the outside world. They say that this energy is dynamic or vital. The right side of the brain (and left side of the body) is concerned with mental activities and the inner world. Yogis say that this energy is mental.

Few of us are perfectly balanced in this respect. One side is usually overactive, and the other side correspondingly suppressed. We are either an extrovert or an introvert, rather than a perfect mixture of both and able to switch from one to the other as needed.

To achieve a balance between inwardness and outwardness, you can practice an exercise called Alternate Nostril Breathing, after the other balancing exercises described above, and with the same rhythm. The right hand is used to close off either one nostril or the other, so it is divided into three parts. The thumb is used to close the right nostril, the two middle fingers rest against the forehead, and the ring and little finger close off the left nostril. The left hand continues to rest in the lap or on the left thigh. You may need to practice a bit to get your breath and right hand coordinated.

When you are ready, breathe out and then close the right nostril. Breathe in through the left. Close the left nostril and open the right, then breathe out through it. When you are ready, breathe in again through the right nostril. Close it and open the left nostril, then breathe out through it. And in through it . . . and out through the right. And in through the right . . . and out through the left. And so on, for a few minutes, or until you feel tired — ending the cycle by breathing out through the left nostril.

When you have mastered this simple technique, you will be able to activate and balance both your vital and your mental energies. You will be amazed how much brighter and more alert you feel.

EXERCISE FIVE
FROM EARTH TO HEAVEN AND BACK

Now it is time to "breathe up the middle of the spine." This is a purely subjective feeling, of course, as air only passes in and out of the lungs. But *energy* can be directed anywhere.

As you breathe in, feel that you are directing your energy from the base of your spine up to the top of your head. As you breathe out, feel that you are taking this energy down again to the base of your spine. Repeat this visualization, synchronized with your breathing, for a few moments.

There are many ways to do this, and also to describe its purpose. We can say that we are balancing "above" with "below," spirit with matter, or heaven with earth. This may seem fanciful — but we all know people who are "too heavenly to be any earthly use," don't we? They need a bit of "earthing." Likewise, we know people who are too materialistic, too "earthbound," who could do with a bit of "uplift." Most of us need to extend our range upon the ladder that leads from earth to heaven and back again.

Many people are quite visual, and have no trouble "seeing" a stream of light moving up and down their spine. Some are more auditory, and find it easier to "hear" a hissing, or a flowing noise like water in a pipe. Others are tactile, and prefer to "feel" a sensation of tingling or buzzing, or warmth or shivers, as they direct energy up and down their spine. Experiment, until you find the best imagery for you.

Until now, the exercises have been preparing you for meditation, getting you in the right frame of mind — balanced and relaxed. This last one, however, is a meditation technique in itself — because it uses posture, breathing and mental focus *together*.

7

A CLASSICAL
TRADITION

PATANJALI'S RAJA YOGA

There are many traditions of meditation, but that
of Patanjali is perhaps one of the easiest for us to
use. Patanjali understood that people differ, and
included something for everyone in his masterly
text.

Patanjali was a great Indian teacher, who brought
together all the best techniques of meditation that
were in use in his day. He is believed to have lived
during the second or third century A.D., although
little is known about him. Georg Feuerstein, in his
Textbook of Yoga, writes: "It is reasonable to assume
that Patanjali was a great authority on Yoga in his
time, and most probably the head of a school
which was philosophically very active."

Patanjali's wisdom is recorded in a work called
The Yoga Sutras of Patanjali, which sets out to
define enlightenment and to explain how this

state can be reached through meditation. The path that he prescribes leads us out of the dark muddle of delusion, confusion and half truths that usually fills our minds. By following this path, we will eventually arrive in the bright daylight of pure consciousness, which will banish our ignorance and replace it with enlightenment.

The path that Patanjali outlines so clearly is the Yoga of meditation, which has traditionally been called the royal path or Raja Yoga. A raja in India is a prince or king. In Patanjali's feudal world, a raja held absolute power, and naturally attracted the brightest and best minds to his court. A wise raja was never too proud to learn from the sages, who could lead him to rulership over his own self. So, by inference, the path of meditation is fit for a king and will make kings and queens of all those who follow it with dedication and perseverance.

THE YOGA OF MEDITATION

How does Patanjali define this state of meditation? Slightly paraphrasing the translation, he says in effect:

Meditation is the settling of the mind into silence. When the mind is settled, we are established in our essential nature . . . (which) is usually overshadowed by the activity of the mind.[1] Mental activity is settled by the practice of meditation . . . (which) will be firmly rooted when it is maintained consistently and with dedication over a long period.[2]

From this we can see that we have to work at it before we can expect our minds to be permanently settled. Luckily, to do this Patanjali gives us many helpful suggestions — which are outlined in this part of the book.

MEDITATION BESTOWS FREEDOM

"The practice of meditation bestows freedom, and is itself the commitment to become established in the state of freedom. . . . Supreme freedom is complete liberation from the world of change."[3] Change will of course continue to occur, since we live in the natural world which never stops changing from moment to moment. However, instead of letting changes upset us and throw us off course, we will understand and use them: "Any change into a new state of being is the result of the fullness of Nature unfolding inherent potential."[4]

Patanjali's philosophy is optimistic. We are all destined to evolve eventually into the ultimate state of freedom where we can "know the unbounded self" — or, in perhaps more familiar terms, "know as we are known." Patanjali assures us that we can help ourselves by "removing the obstacles to natural growth, as a farmer clears the ground for his crops."[5]

THE DEEPER STATE OF MEDITATION

"To begin with, the settled state of mind is accompanied by mental activity. . . After the repeated experience of the settling and ceasing of mental activity comes another state of mind."[6] . . . "This deeper state of meditation is preceded by trust, perseverance, recollection, tranquillity and wisdom."[7]

Patanjali then lists many of the techniques of meditation that will be discussed later in this book. What works for one person may not be right for another — some people respond best to visual imagery, others to sound, others to the sense of touch, and others to combinations of all three. Some people are more in touch with their bodies, others with their emotions and still others with their minds. Patanjali realized that no single technique, however excellent, can suit everybody.

"Then the mind will turn inwards and the obstacles which stand in the way of progress will disappear . . . They are distractions from the path of meditation. Such distractions make the body restless, the breathing coarse and the mind agitated. They result in suffering."[8]

THE NINE DISTRACTIONS

These bear a remarkable resemblance to the adverse effects of stress or imbalance, as described in the previous chapter. However, they take us even further down the slippery slope toward imprisonment in our "lower nature," and away from our climb towards "supreme freedom." They are listed by Patanjali in the following order:

• "Illness"

• "Fatigue"

• "Doubt" (also translated as "lack of enthusiasm")

• "Carelessness"

• "Laziness"

• "Attachment" (also translated as "craving for pleasure" and "worldly-mindedness")

• "Delusion" (also translated as "false perception of one's own powers")

• "Failure to achieve the deeper state of meditation" (also translated as "despair caused by failure to concentrate")

• "Failure to maintain the deeper state of meditation"[9]

Patanjali tells us that this slippery slope can be avoided, and these nine distractions eliminated, through the techniques of meditation — such as concentration on a single focus, cultivating the qualities of the heart and through the practice of various breathing exercises.

Clearly there is nothing truly new under the sun — stress due to environmental pollution, bombardment of information through the media and the pace of modern living may be recent phenomena, but all the other "distractions" that make us feel ill and dispirited, or that take us away from our chosen path, have always been with us. And so has the cure for most of them. We can use the ancient tried and proven ways to make us balanced and whole. These techniques involve the use of our bodies, minds and hearts.

[1] Alistair Shearer, *Effortless Being*, London: Wildwood House 1982 (translation of Patanjali's *Yoga Sutras*) Chapter 1, v. 2–4.

[2] Ibid., Chapter 1, v. 12–14.

[3] Ibid., Chapter 1, v. 14–16.

[4] Ibid., Chapter 4, v. 2.

[5] Ibid., Chapter 4, v. 3.

[6] Ibid., Chapter 1, v. 17–18.

[7] Ibid., Chapter 1, v. 20.

[8] Ibid., Chapter 1, v. 29–31.

[9] Ibid., Chapter 1, v. 30.

FOCUSING THE MIND

KEEPING THE MIND ON THE JOB

Finding an upright seated position — and working to maintain and improve it — requires concentration. It is so easy to forget to keep the head in line, the sternum lifted, the waist back and the coccyx tucked under, all at the same time. After a while, the pose — in all its detail — becomes second nature. The same degree of concentration is no longer required, so the mind starts to wander.

You suddenly become aware that you are making lists in your mind of things you plan to do later on, or that you are recalling a time that has passed, or that you are daydreaming about somewhere far away. You have lost the immediacy of being in the here and now.

HERE AND NOW

The immediacy of here and now has been lost, yet this is the only place and time in which any of us can actually experience living. All other places and times can exist, for us, only in our imaginations.

Meditation trains us to keep our minds on the job in hand, on what is happening here and now. Suppose we were all actors playing a part on the stage of life. Wouldn't we be better actors if we remained focused on what we were doing and saying, if we could get ourselves right into our parts and stay in them totally — rather than writing shopping lists in our heads at the same time? It is crucial to find ways to stop our minds from wandering away from the job in hand.

"KEEPING THE MIND IN THE BODY"

To begin with, the mind is kept busy remembering all the details of the meditation posture. After some time, these details will become engraved on your memory. Your mind gradually feeds them into the "computer," or on to "automatic pilot," leaving you free to think about other things — and so you do. The mental chattering, which meditation practice is designed to silence, has started up again. What can you do to stop it? The answer is to "Keep your mind in your body."

You are working on posture, so every time your mind slinks off to play truant from the job in hand you gently recall it. There is always something within your body that you can focus on. You may feel the weight of parts of your body pressing on to other parts, or against your cushion or chair. You may notice your heart beating, or your digestion rumbling. You may not feel as stretched upward as you were to begin with, becoming conscious of the constant effect of gravity upon the body. Keeping your mind in your body gives it considerable freedom of movement, and at the same time, firmly marked limits.

It is a fascinating meditation exercise simply to watch the tricks your mind will play in order to escape from the job at hand. The mind is watching the mind — which illustrates how divided our minds are. There are a whole crowd of "minds" within the head of each one of us.

Keeping the mind in the body is a simple exercise that will teach you a lot about yourself. It will also develop your ability to concentrate. Unfortunately, many of us avoided learning how to concentrate during our school years, and have never learned this skill since. As a result, it has always been harder than it needs to be to learn new skills. Concentration is the first prerequisite for study of any subject.

Keeping the Mind on the Breath

Concentration on your breathing is the next stage, as you work your way through the sequence of breathing exercises. There is plenty to observe, and variety as well, as you spend a few minutes on each exercise and then move on to the next. Eventually you will have balanced the breath in the upper and lower part of the lungs, and the length of time you take to breathe in and to breathe out, and through the left and the right nostrils.

The last breathing exercise was to breathe up and down the middle of the spine. At this point, your body (the physical breathing process), your energy (which is being moved up and down your spine) and your mind (which is directing this flow) are all working in unison. You should be feeling calm, balanced and happy.

Just "Being"

Now is the time to stop directing the flow of energy, and just to "be." Your mind is relaxed, still and silent. This is the state of meditation, out of which all healing changes will arise. But in no time at all your mind is off again, as busy as ever. Don't despair at this point — this is the natural behavior of the human mind. So how can you "control" it?

This is the wrong question, based on the wrong attitude. Trying to control your mind through sheer will-power will bring conflict, not success — rather like when you try to control other people. What you are trying to do instead is to train your mind to enjoy being focused and still for longer and longer periods. It is rather like dealing with a small child — when your mind wanders off, give it a new focus and it will come trotting back quite happily. Don't expect too much at first, but build up gradually.

One thing you can do is to go back to the beginning of your practice, and work through it all again. This is the best solution when you are still learning the exercises and do not yet want to go further. Once posture and breathing exercises have become second nature, you are ready to learn a new practice, which will bring your mind back into focus.

There are many excellent concentration exercises that can induce the state of meditation.

EXERCISE SIX
"A SHOWER OF ENERGY"

You have been moving energy up and down your spine, as in Exercise Five. Then you paused, just to "be," but now you have become aware that your mind has wandered off somewhere.

You call your mind back gently and take it on an inner exploration, a journey around your body, checking for tension anywhere, or discomfort of any kind. When you have found a part that could do with a "shower of energy" you breathe in, up through the spine as before. Think of the energy traveling up under pressure, as through a hose pipe.

As you breathe out, you release this pressure, as a shower of energy which washes through the part that needs healing, causing it to relax and absorb this extra energy. Tensions and discomfort are washed away. Picture the energy flowing — perhaps as a stream of white or golden light. Make the "shower" look beautiful, like a fountain catching glints of rainbow colors. Feel that it is healing, relaxing, restorative. Repeat this visualization with every breath, drawing the energy up under pressure as you breathe in, and releasing it in a healing shower as you breathe out.

You may have no particular area that needs attention. In this case, bathe your whole self in the healing shower of light each time you breathe out. After a few such breaths stop, and once again just "be."

The practices of meditation have many great benefits, but their sole purpose is to bring you to the state of meditation where you are able to quietly *do nothing* except be totally receptive. Therefore it is important to refrain from getting caught up in the practices themselves, however delightful your visualizations may be.

Remember the "distractions" that Patanjali wrote about. "Delusion" — or "false perception of one's own powers" — can trap us very easily in glamorous visualizations that distract us from the true purpose of meditation. Visualizations are no more than a good way for some people to bring themselves to stillness of body, mind and heart. Do not get caught up in them, but use them to help you to reach the state of meditation.

EXERCISE SEVEN
CANDLE GAZING

For this concentration exercise you will need to get prepared in advance, before you sit for meditation. You will need a darkened, draft-free room — so that you can see the candle flame easily, and so that it does not flicker. The candle should be fixed in a large saucer, lighted, and placed on a stool or table so that the burning wick is at eye level and about an arm's length away from you when you are seated for meditation. It is important that you do not have to move either your eyes or your head to look at the candle flame, because that would defeat the object of achieving total stillness. So take time to place the candle, and yourself in relation to it.

If you wear glasses, you may leave them on or take them off — but it is important to arrange yourself so that you see one image, not two.

Note: *This exercise is not recommended for people who suffer from epilepsy or migraines.*

When you are seated, attend to your body as usual, getting yourself relaxed, and the trunk well positioned for good breathing. Practice lengthening the outbreath for a few moments. Then look at the candle, keeping your eyes still. Your gaze should be soft, not staring — almost as though you were dreamily looking through the flame just where it comes out of the wick, blue turning to orange. Avoid blinking as much as you can.

It is said that mental and physical energies work together, so stillness of the body — especially the eyeballs — quickly brings stillness of the mind. This unblinking gaze may cause your eyes to water quite quickly. You can leave them open if you wish, letting the tears flow, which may make you feel sad for no particular reason. Most of us have not allowed ourselves to cry enough, although tears are very healing. So cry, if you want to, gazing calmly at the candle flame through your tears. Weep contentedly, even if you think you have nothing to cry about. It is not always necessary to know why you feel like crying, or to have some "proper reason" for letting go of old, perhaps forgotten, sadness.

If crying disturbs you, then close your eyes as soon as they begin to water. You will see an after-image of the flame against your closed eyelids. You can continue gazing at this, just as you did at the actual candle. As the image fades, open your eyes and continue gazing at the candle as before.

This exercise should be done for about five minutes to begin with, before stopping just to "be." You can build up to ten or fifteen minutes, but that is long enough.

Remain in the ensuing stillness until you notice that your mind has become active again. Then take plenty of time to "come out" of meditation. Sit quietly, and watch your breathing. Then become fully aware of your body, before stretching and getting up.

EXERCISE EIGHT
OUTER AND INNER SOUNDS

Many people go "inward" more easily through listening than through looking — especially if there are various sounds to listen to. It is good to sit outside in a garden or park the first few times that you do the following exercise. Be sure you are warmly dressed, however, so that you will not be distracted by feeling cold.

Sit in a suitable position, checking the erect posture of your spine and the relaxed state of your limbs. Lengthen the out-breath for a few moments. Then *open your ears*. Passively receive every sound that comes to you, without considering what might be causing it. The mind should be off duty — only the ears are working. Pick up first the loudest sounds, then the quieter ones, then the quietest of all.

Then bring your listening attention *inside* your body. What can you hear? Your heartbeat? Your breathing? Your digestion? Just pick up these sounds, without effort. Be as passive as a radio picking up sounds from the airwaves.

One day you may hear your own inner sound. It may be a high-pitched hum, rather like standing beneath telephone wires, or listening to the vibration coming from a refrigerator. Or it may be lower, like the roar of a distant sea. Or it may be tinkling, like the sound of bells. It may tick like an old treadle sewing machine. All these are traditional descriptions, except that the old texts spoke of conch shells and crickets chirping, and not of electrical or mechanical noises that may be more familiar to us.

Being able to hear your special inner sound is a great gift, because it gives you your own personal meditation focus from that moment on. Unlike the sounds of tinnitus, it never intrudes: you hear it only when you stay very quiet and listen for it. Behind the first sound — the high-pitched electrical sound — lie the others. As you listen ever more intently, you may pick them up. Each new sound is a gift in itself, and a barometer of the deepening of your inner silence.

As with the "seeing" meditations, these "listening" techniques should be practiced for five minutes or so at first. The time can be gradually lengthened, as you relax into greater stillness. Come out slowly, grounding yourself first in your breath and then in your body, before making any movement.

EXERCISE NINE
THE SOUND OF THE BREATH

Traditionally, the breath makes a sound: SO as you breathe in, and HAM as you breathe out. It is quite easy to imagine that you can hear these sounds as you breathe up and down your spine. For some people, it is easier to focus on the breath by listening to these sounds, as well as (or instead of) "seeing" energy as a stream of light.

SO-HAM is a mantra, or sacred sound, that connects the person who uses it with the divine source. Such mantras cannot really be translated. However, SO-HAM does have a traditional meaning: *Sah* means He the Supreme; *Aham* means I the individual soul. So energy can be thought of as streaming between the universal self and the individual self, bringing them together into one. If this idea appeals to you, use the mantra SO-HAM. If it does not feel right for you, do not use it.

The meaning and use of mantra is discussed in detail in Chapter 12.

9

PRELIMINARY
ATTITUDES

THE THREE PRACTICAL STEPS

Patanjali starts his chapter on the practices that lead
to the state of meditation by describing the three
essential "preliminary purificatory practices," without which we cannot hope to succeed. He says:
"Purification, refinement, surrender — these are
the practical steps on the path of (Raja) Yoga."[1]

Another translation of the same verse says:
"Austerity, self-study and resignation to God constitute preliminary (Raja) Yoga."[2] Yet another
translation puts it this way: "Accepting pain as
purification, study of spiritual books, and surrender to the Supreme Being constitute (Raja) Yoga
in practice."[3] Sanskrit is a language with many
shades of meaning, so it is always helpful to com-
pare several translations to get the full flavor of
what is being taught.

One thing is quite clear, however: Raja Yoga, the
path of meditation, involves all our faculties. We

are to be physically active and disciplined, we are to use our minds to see ourselves and our world more clearly, and we are to give away, gladly and willingly, all that we have labored to gain. What we keep for ourselves remains barren. Only by "surrendering" it all can it become fruitful — like the grain of wheat that must die in the ground before it can sprout into new and abundant life.

We are not expected to achieve perfection in these three preliminary steps before we can move on, or hope to reach the state of meditation, for we learn as we travel along this path. However, we do need to appreciate the importance of these steps from the outset — even if we are not very good at practicing them.

It may be helpful to call them fundamental attitudes rather than steps. An attitude is something we always have, whatever we may be doing, thinking or feeling — and whether or not we are conscious of it. So, the more we learn to replace our habitual attitudes with the ones prescribed by Patanjali, the more we will be able to abide in the state of meditation, the deeper this state will become, and the closer we will get to enlightenment.

These three attitudes are the essential preparation for the state of meditation — self-discipline, self-knowledge and self-surrender.

In his next verse, Patanjali explains that these "practical and preliminary" attitudes "weaken the causes of suffering" which delay our evolution, and that they "nourish the state of deep meditation."[4] These three attitudes will in fact make us successful in anything we undertake in life — they are the basis of all progress, material or spiritual.

SELF-DISCIPLINE

It is self-discipline that makes us regular in our practice of meditation, or playing the piano, or learning a language. We must practice regularly to learn any skill, whether we feel in the mood to do so or not. People who only practice when they feel like it will remain forever amateurs.

If we have to study early in the morning we must get up in time, and refrain from going to bed late. If we want to keep fit, we must exercise our muscles and refrain from eating too much. Self-discipline usually involves making the effort to do something specific, as well as refraining from doing those things that are counter-productive.

The Sanskrit word used by Patanjali has been translated in many ways — austerity, accepting pain as purification, controlling our physical appetites and passions, burning effort, zeal, the science of character building. Self-discipline encompasses most of these meanings.

For meditation, the most important aspect is regularity of practice, and continued commitment and enthusiasm even when things are not going well.

SELF-KNOWLEDGE

The ancient Greek philosophers taught: "Know yourself and you will know the universe." They had the motto "Know yourself" inscribed in the temple of Delphi, which was called by the Greeks the "navel (or center) of the world."[5]

Most of us have only a vague idea of what goes on inside either our bodies or our minds. Yet universal laws operate within us, as within everything else. By observing these laws at work in ourselves we can learn to recognize them for what they are, no matter where they appear. We no longer feel ourselves to be standing apart from the rest of nature, since we follow the same laws and flow to the same cosmic rhythms.

This brings new responsibility. We can no longer blame others for everything unpleasant that happens to us — for we are part of that happening. If we want to change things we must start with ourselves — our own separatist beliefs, our self-centeredness, our defensive attitudes. This in turn will alter the way the world interacts with us. "As you sow, so shall you reap."

Changing the world starts with ourselves. Our nightly review of each day's events, and especially the habit of keeping a spiritual diary that reflects how we respond to things and people closest to us, will prove to be real eye-openers.

Perhaps our closest relatives have been criticizing us for years about particular "failings." Probably all that this has achieved is to make us feel uncomfortable, resentful, undervalued or guilty. It seldom improves our behavior, because we must observe it for ourselves before we can take it seriously and make the effort to change it.

Many of the new psychotherapeutic techniques that are now so popular are aimed at providing us with a clear picture of ourselves in a supportive and loving framework. We gradually come to accept that we are as we are — frightened, rebellious, immature, or whatever it may be. We are gently led to realize that these are simply childish reactions that we can afford to relinquish now that we are at last "growing up."

Love helps us to unfold into our potential, so it is vital that the attention that we give to ourselves and to our present shortcomings should always be loving and encouraging.

Patanjali's word for self-knowledge has another meaning as well. It can be translated as self-study, and also as the study of scriptures or sacred writings. Here Patanjali departs radically from most of the psychotherapeutic techniques that are currently popular, and which strenuously avoid what are called value judgments. It is true that we may not want, or trust, a dictatorial therapist who tries to "convert" us to a particular moral tradition. But we do need *something*. Excellence is helped by example.

We must have a standard to work toward. There is no point in seeing ourselves as we are unless we have some idea of how we could be. The teachings and poetry of great saints and sages are wonderfully uplifting and inspiring, and can be very helpful in this regard. To read them in bed makes the best possible end to the day, and ensures that our next day will be that much better. They also make comparisons pointless. Unless we are lucky enough to know such a saint personally, we can truly say: "The difference between the best and the worst of us is as nothing, compared with the difference between how we are and how we are meant to become."

We started with self-discipline, the first "preliminary attitude" on the path of meditation. Success here is entirely up to us — we have to make it work for ourselves, to make time and take trouble over our meditation techniques on a regular basis.

Meditation is often criticized — by those who do not practice it — as a very self-centered occupation. So it is, at this stage. We also have to work hard at acquiring self-knowledge, through observing ourselves without judgment, and accepting what we find. This too can be seen as a self-centered occupation — and as self-indulgent and narcissistic. "All that pre-occupation with your own psyche!" exclaim those people who would often prefer you to be pre-occupied with theirs.

Half-way through looking at the concept of self-knowledge, however, everything suddenly changes. Here is Patanjali, telling us to study the sacred scriptures of the world, and to set ourselves standards to aim for. What are these sacred scriptures likely to be concerned with? Whatever their source, they probably speak of God, of the relationship between God and each individual human person, and of the unconditional love that should exist between each of us and every other person we come into contact with.

Our efforts may seem rather futile in the face of such a vast challenge. Yet that is precisely where we must start. . . . Where will our journey end? Patanjali tells us bluntly enough — with self-surrender.

SELF-SURRENDER

Again, the Sanskrit phrase that Patanjali uses can be translated in several ways — surrendering to the Supreme Being, resignation to God, the dedication of the fruits of one's works to God, devotion to the Lord, etc.

We may think that we do not believe in God, or that we do not worship any so-called Lord. But in fact we do all worship something. Where your treasure is, there will your heart be also. What in life do you treasure most? In the West it is often our independence of thought — we worship the power of the mind, and the freedom to think as we please.

This is clearly a very different form of freedom from that which can be glimpsed through meditation. In Patanjali's philosophy, the mind is part of the natural world — changeable and therefore less than the highest, unchanging reality. He says that reality is "pure consciousness," which is universal and therefore cannot be the property of any individual creature.

Are we ready to give up our own egotistical freedoms to acquire the freedom to be part of all that truly is? Self-surrender is an affair of the heart, of wanting something so much that you will give up everything else — even your own ego — to acquire this treasure.

There seems to be a scale of freedoms, from the most petty to the most exalted. We already know that meditation requires self-discipline, and that we must therefore value it enough to be prepared to practice it regularly. We may have to give up the freedom to sleep late in the morning, or some other freedom that we also value. Do we value our chosen path more than the freedom to do as we please during the time we have set aside for meditation?

It is all a matter of priorities. We want to sleep late, we want to keep up our regular practice, we want to make an urgent telephone call just when we had planned to meditate. Which do we want most? Whichever it is, that is what we shall find ourselves doing.

Modern life is so frenetic for most of us simply because there are so many things claiming our time, energy and attention. It is more important than ever to prioritize — and to make sure that the precious time needed to develop our own inner potential is not squeezed out of our lives.

There is a famous Indian parable: A man had many small thorns in his feet, which hurt him as he walked barefoot through the jungle. So in order to remove them, he found a really big thorn, and with it he dug all the little ones out of his feet. The thorns represent all the desires that we pick up as we tread the path of life through the jungle of the world. In order to get rid of them, we must desire some one thing so much that all the rest no longer matter.

Here is another story. A young Indian girl was running swiftly along the road to meet her lover. She could think of nothing else but him, and of how happy she would be when they met. In her absentminded haste she ran across the edge of a prayer mat, belonging to a priest who had settled down to meditate by the roadside.

The priest stood up furiously and shook his fist at the girl. "You careless and disrespectful young hussy!" he thundered. "What are you thinking of, to disturb a priest who is meditating upon God?"

The girl retorted pertly: "If you were thinking about your God as intently as I was thinking about my lover, you would never have noticed that I trod on your prayer mat."

We worship what is most important to us personally. It may be sex, or love, or financial security. It may be status, fame, or freedom to do as we please. It may be creativity, variety, self-development, or contact with God. It may also change, as we change and mature. Whatever it is, it provides the hidden motivation behind all that we do. We need this same motivation to keep us on the royal path of meditation despite all the "little thorns" of desire that distract us. We also need to remove some of these distractions by sitting down quietly and sorting out our priorities.

Self-surrender sounds harsh and painful, while surrendering yourself to your heart's desire has a different ring to it — yearning and bittersweet. To realize that they are both the same, it is necessary to find out what it is that you desire, and to recognize the hidden motivations within.

Self-discipline, self-understanding and self-surrender develop together through physical, mental and emotional meditation practices.

[1] Alistair Shearer, *Effortless Being*, London: Wildwood House 1982, Chapter 2, v. 1.

[2] I. K. Taimni, *The Science of Yoga*, Theosophical Publishing House 1961.

[3] Swami Satchidananda, *Integral Yoga*, Integral Yoga Publications, USA 1978.

[4] Alistair Shearer, *Effortless Being*, London: Wildwood House 1982, Chapter 2, v. 2.

[5] *The Oxford Dictionary of Quotations*, 2nd Edition, Oxford University Press 1954.

10

RE-BALANCING

BALANCING THE MATERIAL AND THE SPIRITUAL ASPECTS

The practice of meditation brings healing through re-balancing those aspects of our total being that have been thrown out of balance for various reasons. None of us is perfectly balanced, and it is for this reason that we need — to use the Buddha's terminology — to tread the Middle Way. This Way passes harmoniously between a series of complementary opposites that are neither good nor bad in themselves. They are harmful to our happiness and evolution when unbalanced, helpful when balanced.

Not everyone who wishes to learn the techniques of meditation is eager to explore the more spiritual aspects of the subject. Some may believe that no God exists — for atheism is a belief like any other. Some are agnostic, maintaining that we cannot possibly know what lies beyond this life.

This was the Buddha's stance, and the reason why Buddhists do not speak of God, but of an unknowable void, which is the revered source of all things. "Beyond, beyond . . . beyond the Great Beyond . . . Beyond even the thought of beyond . . . Homage to Thee!"[1] This translation of a famous Buddhist mantra, known as the heart sutra, expresses perfectly the reverence we can feel for what we cannot know.

One thing seems certain: intellectual speculation about, and comparisons of, the great religions may clear our minds but will not bring us any nearer to a personal relationship with the spiritual pole of our being. We can "use the mind to go beyond the mind," as in the meditation techniques already discussed in this book, but beyond that point only the heart can take us. If we do not exercise our spiritual heart, we will remain out of balance and stuck in that materialism which modern life thrusts at us constantly. This imbalance can cause more unrecognized stress that any other source of stress.

Let us go back through the exercises suggested up to now, to see which imbalances they are designed to address and what kind of healing they can bring about.

RE-BALANCING THROUGH THE MEDITATION POSTURE

This involves achieving a balance between being grounded and rising up (see Chapter 5). It is rather like placing a ladder correctly, so that it is safe to use. If the ground is uneven, or not solid, it will fail to support the ladder. We can indulge in all the fantasies that we please, but they cannot become reality without suitable preparation or groundwork. Our dreams will come tumbling round our ears when our ladder falls, through lack of attention to the ground upon which it rests. This is a very common occurrence, especially among young and inexperienced people who have great ambitions but have not yet learned that all success depends upon thorough preparation — the groundwork of Patanjali's first "preliminary attitude," self-discipline. From this firm base it becomes possible to reach upward.

The opposite to being too flighty is to be too much of a stick in the mud. This leads to refusing to believe that improvement — or change of any sort — is either possible or desirable. It is quite usual to veer between one of these imbalances and its opposite. After years of youthful and impractical enthusiasm, we may become old at heart, cynical and world-weary. Of course, it is easier to blame unspecific others than to admit our own imbalances, and then do something to correct them. One of the greatest healing gifts of meditation is that it gives us the opportunity — and brings us to the point where we are ready to do so — to look honestly at ourselves and accept what we see.

We cannot be free in any real sense if we are enslaved by one of a pair of opposites and averse to the other. Freedom is being poised *between* them, to use either as appropriate.

A study of the meditation postures can teach us a great deal, as we reflect upon what they all have in common — the solid base, the uprising spine, the clear head resting lightly on top. The whole attitude is both alert and relaxed, poised between activity and passivity.

This is another complementary pair of opposites usually out of balance in our daily lives. Many of us have been brought up to feel that we are a waste of space unless we are busy doing something supposedly useful. So we scurry around from morning till night, refusing to allow our systems to come back to balance through regular periods of passivity. Passivity is seen as feebleness and lack of vigor. The devil may indeed find work for idle hands to do, but God has a hard time communicating with us if we are always too busy — or too exhausted — to listen.

The other side of the coin is that type of passivity that can only be spiritual when in isolation. There are some people who fall apart when they have to come out of their ivory tower and live among the rest of us. Buddhists stress the importance of both retreating from the world and then coming back to it, for it is in the market place that the lessons learned on the mountain are actually put into practice.

Watching the breath (see Exercise One, Chapter 6, pages 40–41) is an example of being both active and passive at the same time. Some muscles are actively maintaining the seated posture, while others — not needed for sitting upright — are relaxed. Some systems of the body are active — the heart and blood vessels, and the muscles used for breathing, for instance. Others are passive, especially the brain and nervous system. The breath is being observed, without thought, comment, opinions or judgement.

Re-balancing Through Deepening the Breath

This is an exercise designed to re-balance the two halves of the autonomic nervous system (see Exercise Two, Chapter 6, pages 41–42). When we perceive something, through any of our five senses, the brain receives the information and decides how best to respond. As far as the autonomic nervous system is concerned, there are only two responses.

If the brain decides that the incoming information spells danger, it switches on the sympathetic branch, whose sole duty is to sympathize with our predicament and help us to get out of it as quickly as possible. As far as the nervous system is concerned, we are still animals controlled by instincts. The dangers that animals perceive are always physical — such things as larger animals who must be either fought or run away from. So the heartbeat is speeded up, we take in big gulps of extra air and our fighting and flight muscles are tightened up ready for action.

When we are actually in physical danger, our priority is obviously short-term survival rather than long-term well-being. All those systems not needed for fight or flight are suppressed for the time being. This system works well throughout nature in the wild: the animal either successfully fights or flees from its enemy, or it gets eaten. If it survives it hides away in a safe place to recover from the ordeal.

Once the danger is perceived to have been dealt with, the brain decides that all is well. It switches off the sympathetic branch of the autonomic nervous system and switches on the parasympathetic branch, which is concerned with long-term well-being. It instigates rest, repair if needed, digestion and absorption — generally re-balancing all the bodily systems of an animal that has been subjected to severe stress.

The nervous systems of human beings remain as they were when we were wild animals — but our hearts and minds have changed, and so have the dangers we have to face. We perceive all kinds of dangers to our survival and well-being that cannot be resolved simply by fighting or running away. Life in the workplace, and in traffic jams, can be exceedingly stressful, aggravated by the feeling that we are trapped in the situation. Money problems, relationship problems, career problems — all these add to our unresolved burden of stress. We also have the capacity — and the tendency — to live in the past and the future as well as in the present, and to be upset by them too.

Unresolved conflicts, dangers that we have neither conquered nor escaped from, will continue to produce stress until we learn how consciously to reverse the processes set in motion by our sympathetic nervous systems. Many experts now believe that most of our ill health is caused by long-term stress.

How can we reverse these processes? Our breathing pattern is one thing we *can* change. When we notice that our breathing is mostly in the upper chest, we realize that we are unconsciously still on red alert. By focusing on deep breathing, which uses the diaphragm, we start to activate those processes governed by the parasympathetic, or "all is well," branch of the autonomic nervous system. Since only one of these branches can be dominant, this means that the red alert button is switched off for the time being.

Balance is being poised between the two modes, slipping from one to the other as required. Imbalance is being stuck in one mode. It is just as unbalanced to be always in a state of depression and lethargy as it is to be constantly overstimulated. This can happen when our stress level becomes too severe to cope with, and the body demands a respite. We have a breakdown in one or other of the body's systems — and an enforced rest.

Making the outbreath longer (see Exercise Three, Chapter 6, pages 42–44) also tells the brain that there is no panic, no need to rush to take in more oxygen, no enemy to fight or flee from. It reinforces the message that we have enough of that most vital of all commodities — oxygen from the air we breathe. People who realize that they have enough — of anything — do not need to put themselves under stress striving to acquire more.

Yet our whole urban, industrial society is based on wanting more. If times are hard and people start to tighten their belts, the government of the day worries, in case economic growth does not reach the targets set. Manufacturers look for new markets in the third world countries. It is clear that perpetual economic growth cannot be sustained forever, and also that life as we know it in the affluent West cannot continue without it.

It is our attitude, our perception of "enough" that has to change to break this vicious circle before it destroys us all. We live in a society that is in a dire state of imbalance between taking and giving back. Simply focusing on giving our used breath back to the universe slowly, and with gratitude, can help us. Our well-being, and even our lives, depend upon the balanced intake and outflow of air. Perhaps our future, and the future of our planet, depend upon this same balance expressed in other ways.

We also require a healthy balance between mental and physical activity. Our society values mental activity more than hands-on labor, so from schooldays onward we are encouraged to use our brains rather than our bodies. Lack of exercise and over-stimulation of our mental energies make many of us very unbalanced. Most of the things that cause us stress, such as worry about the future or anger and resentment about things in the past, are mental rather than physical. Balancing the left and right sides of the brain by practicing Alternate Nostril Breathing (see Exercise Four, Chapter 6, pages 44–45) can help us here.

Re-balancing Our Earth and Heaven Poles

Exercise Five, Chapter 6 (see page 46), brings us right back to the beginning of this chapter. It is also probably as far as we can go without introducing a spiritual element into our practice of meditation. Talk of heaven may not suit those who like to keep their religion in a quite separate compartment from the rest of their lives.

There is no cause for alarm — yet. Exercises Six, Seven and Eight, Chapter 8 (see pages 55–59), are not in any way religious. Later in this book, we will look at some more psychological ideas, in connection with the chakras, or energy wheels. These ideas, like the ones introduced so far, can also help us with Patanjali's second "preliminary attitude," self-knowledge — without involving us in either sacred scriptures or self-surrender.

You may think that the simple meditation techniques referred to above cannot make a difference. In one way this is correct. Five or ten minutes here and there is neither here nor there, in terms of its possible beneficial effects. But five or ten minutes of re-balancing, followed by a few moments of mental stillness, can make a tremendous difference when practiced every day, morning and evening. It can change our whole outlook on life — and many people have testified to this fact.

Exercise Nine, Chapter 8 (see pages 59–60), involves mantra. As explained before, any mantra is always sacred sound. For many people, the use of mantra in their meditation practice is the most transforming technique of all.

---

[1] Ram Dass (tr.), *Gatay Gatay*, Paragatay, Parasamgatay, Bodhi Svaha. Private pamphlet given to students on retreat.

PART THREE

—

GOING
DEEPER

11

CHANGING ATTITUDES

WALKING THE TIGHTROPE

So far our meditation practice has been leading us into ever greater balance and a stillness that is filled with life. We are, for brief moments, poised in that state of meditation which Patanjali describes as "the settled mind." We may even be able to return to it, quickly re-balancing ourselves when we realize that we have got stuck in either the frenzied activity of red alert or its opposite, depressed exhaustion. "All is well" is the conviction that comes to us when we are feeling neither threatened nor in urgent need of rest and repair.

Mother Julian of Norwich, a medieval Christian mystic, spent a large part of her life in meditation. Through her own experiences, she was able to write, with absolute certainty: "All will be well, and all will be well, and every manner of thing will be well." [1] We will know and feel this when we are able to achieve, and to remain in, the state of balance which Patanjali calls the "settled mind." From there we may progress to the "deeper state" which he describes.

Imagine being a tightrope walker on the high wire. You appear, to the onlookers down below, to be absolutely still and totally in command of the forces of gravity. It all looks so easy. There you are, perfectly centered and able to move any way you please. You know, however, that getting to this peak of performance comes only after a great deal of practice. You probably spent a great deal of time trying to balance on much lower, thicker wires, until you learned to find — and to remain in — your own "center." You learned how to move effortlessly, saving your will-power for the discipline of sticking to regular practice — and then relaxing into it.

Any feat of balance involves the will to do it and the ability to relax while you are doing it. It is much the same with meditation — regular practice of the techniques brings the reward of finding your own center of balance between all the complementary pairs of opposites that threaten to upset your equilibrium. You also learn, with practice, how to re-balance yourself when one or other of these opposites pulls you away from your center.

MORPHIC RESONANCE

For a time, the attempt to become and to stay centered will probably occupy all your attention. But eventually you will wonder: "Where can I go from here? How can I use what I have gained to help other people or myself?" These are of course enormous questions. The first comment to make is that your centeredness *already* helps both others and your-self far more than you may realize. The biochemist, Rupert Sheldrake, introduced the concept of morphic resonance to describe the subtle influence that the learning of new skills — by one animal, one person, one tribe or one community — can have upon the rest of the species. It makes it easier for others to learn the new skill. When a certain proportion of the species have learned it, a critical mass is reached. From then on, every member of the species knows the new skill, even if they have never been taught it or live in remote areas away from any contact with the rest of their kind.

Rupert Sheldrake says:

Morphic resonance is the process whereby similar patterns of activity resonate with other similar patterns through or across space and time. The result of this is a kind of collective memory on which all members of the species draw and to which all contribute. So in the biological realm it means that giraffes, for example, all tap in, through morphic resonance, to previous giraffes, through a collective giraffe memory. In the realm of form this gives them their shapes as they develop, and in the realm of behavior, it gives them their characteristic instincts, which are like habits of the species.[2]

This implies that every person who learns to live his or her own life from the center is influencing humanity as a whole, and helping to build up a critical mass that will eventually change the nature of our species.

Your self-discipline, doing your meditation regularly for your own physical, mental and emotional health and balance, actually makes it easier for other people to heal and re-balance themselves. This gives the lie to accusations that meditation is a purely self-centered occupation.

What is the next step, once we have learned to balance reasonably well on our tightrope between the pairs of opposites?

WIDENING THE CENTER

Once we are balanced at our own center we can start to look outward. This can also be put another way: by looking outward we can help to balance our own center. Nature is *one*, and its oneness can be described as the constantly changing interaction between its many different parts.

Patanjali says a lot about our attitudes to other people in his *Yoga Sutras*. Christianity and Buddhism both stress the importance of acknowledging that we belong within a wider framework, that places as much importance upon every other being as upon each individual self. Refusing to accept this view has probably caused more selfishness, violence, misery, and destruction than anything else. Neither aggressors nor victims can find peace and happiness until they spread their attention and love beyond their own selves.

Patanjali's Raja Yoga, or Yoga of Meditation, is aimed at first "settling the mind into silence," then achieving "the deeper states" of meditation, and finally arriving at "enlightenment." We shall then "fulfill the purpose of evolution." By means of that "pure unbounded consciousness" that is released from illusion, we shall see and know for ourselves that all nature rests in its "original state of harmony."[3] The great King David of Israel sang: "Be still, then, and know that I am God."[4]

Once we stop "telling God how to run His world," and accept that "He knows what He is doing," we can shed all manner of stress — and distress. Instead of hindering God by railing against all the "mistakes" that He seems to be making, we can get on with helping Him — by working with rather than against His divine plan.

THE QUALITIES OF THE HEART

Patanjali says: "The mind becomes clear and serene when the qualities of the heart are cultivated. Friendliness towards the joyful, compassion towards the suffering, happiness towards the pure, and impartiality towards the impure."[5]

"Friendliness towards the joyful?" A more common reaction is envy and backbiting. But, of course, if we see ourselves as all parts of one whole, we are glad that there is joy in that whole. "I'm so pleased for you" is the natural reaction — as pleased as I would be if I had occasion to be joyful myself. Joy is an attitude that is present within the whole always — it is there for us to resonate with, thereby increasing the sum total of joy in the world.

"Compassion toward the suffering" is not at all the same as pity or even sympathy — those qualities that can be so unwelcome to the recipients. If any one being in the world hurts, then we are all affected by that suffering. Compassion is simply recognizing, once again, our oneness — feeling with rather than feeling sorry for. Inevitably it is easier to feel with someone who is in a situation you yourself have experienced, because then you know it from the inside. This is why self-help groups, such as Alcoholics Anonymous, are so healing and supportive.

"Happiness toward the pure" can be a hard one! We are far more apt to feel defensive, small and inadequate, guilty and resentful — even positively spiteful — toward those who are holier than we feel. People who have really labored hard and long to divest themselves, in true humility, of the impurities of self-centeredness, however, never present themselves as pure. Purity is a quality that is most often found in people with no pretensions whatsoever, people who do not aspire to shine at anything, people who simply do their best, people who unknowingly glow with love. It is worth seeking out such people. Their company and their example give us hope.

"Impartiality toward the impure" is harder still. St. Paul said: "Be not deceived; God is not mocked: for whatsoever a man soweth, that shall he also reap."[6] Eastern philosophy embraces *karma* — the idea that whatever you send out will come back to you in one form or another, in this life or the next — until *you* interrupt the cycle by forgiveness. This releases both you and the person who has wronged you, and whom you would otherwise, in turn, find yourself harming in the future. Forgiveness, compassion, magnanimity — all these set up a new cycle, a virtuous rather than a vicious one.

What about law and order? What about rewarding good behavior and punishing bad behavior? We should, of course, "hate the sin" so that we are not tempted to fall into it ourselves — but there is seldom agreement about what is, or is not, sinful. All ages and cultures have agreed in principle that people should "do as they wish to be done by," but have had very different ideas about how this should be achieved.

We should not let our condemnation of the sin stop us from loving the sinner — for "There but for the grace of God, go I."[7] It is for God to punish sin. It is for Him to appoint suitable people to carry out His will in this respect.

MEDITATION OF LOVING KINDNESS

This is a famous Buddhist meditation practice, which can be done alone or in a group (see Chapter 15, "Group Meditation").

First of all, sit, relax and balance the breath. Then bring your attention to your heart area — known as putting your mind in your heart. Feel that you are breathing in and out of this space. As you breathe in, say: "May I be well." As you breathe out, say: "May others be well." Continue with this for some time, "attuning yourself to that which is loving and compassionate in the universe."[8]

Next, lengthen and focus on the outbreath. Visualize your parents, either separately or together, and say to yourself: "May they be well." (It does not matter whether or not they are still alive.) Feel kindness and acceptance toward them. Repeat: "May I be well" on the inbreath.

Then visualize your spiritual teachers, saying on the outbreath: "May they be well." Feel gratitude toward them. Repeat: "May I be well" on the inbreath.

In the same way, visualize in turn each member of your family with affection and caring. Then special friends. Then neighbors and colleagues. Then the beautiful Earth, as seen from outer space. Then vastness, emptiness — "May all beings be well."

Return to your own heart — "May I be well."

Now bring to mind someone, alive or dead, that you have hurt in some way. Breathe out and, using their name, say: "Please forgive me." Keep your heart open, and bring to mind someone who has injured you. Breathe out and, using their name, say: "I forgive you . . . You are forgiven . . ." Stay with these feelings of caring.

Return to "May I be well," breathing in and feeling energized and healed. And "May others be well," breathing out through your heart for them.

<hr>

[1] Brendan Doyle, *Meditations with Julian of Norwich*, New Mexico, USA: Bear & Co. 1983, p. 48.

[2] Rupert Sheldrake, speaking to Dan Menkin in an interview in *Quest* magazine, Theosophical Society Autumn 1995.

[3] Alistair Shearer, *Effortless Being*, London: Wildwood House 1982, Chapter 4, v. 32–4.

[4] Ibid., Chapter 1, v. 33.

[5] The Psalms, 46:10, *The Bible*, Authorized Version.

[6] St. Paul, *Epistle to the Galatians* (Authorized Version), 6:7.

[7] Exclaimed by John Bradford in the sixteenth century, on seeing some criminals taken to execution.

[8] This meditation is described in detail by Venerable Anando in *Seeing the Way*, England: Amaravati Publications 1989.

12

SELF-KNOWLEDGE

HUMAN NATURE AND SUBTLE ENERGIES

We can learn a great deal about how we "tick," and human nature generally, through discovering and working with our own inner energies. This is a very direct path to Patanjali's "self-knowledge." It helps us to recognize and change parts of ourselves that are over or underactive, and to resolve and heal deep-seated difficulties, through redistributing, unblocking and re-balancing our "subtle energies."

Study, discussion and meditation that uses the imagery of the chakras can be a very effective way to enhance self-knowledge. The chakras are wheels or vortices of energy that can be seen clairvoyantly or in deep states of meditation. Their balance or imbalances affect us at every level of our being. They cannot be properly appreciated merely by reading the theories about them — fascinating as such a study can be. It is necessary to work with a teacher, who experiences chakra energies as a reality, if you wish to get deeply into this theory and practice. There are, however, many useful visualizations that can be used in meditation to sensitize yourself to these energies. Sound can also help to heighten your awareness.

In the Indian tradition of the Yoga of energies, whose purpose is to prepare the human being for the deepest states of meditation, it is said that each of us consists of five interpenetrating layers called sheaths, or bodies. These need to be aligned and brought into a state of mutual harmony and balance, so that we can be healed, whole, or holy.

The Indian literature on this type of Yoga is very ancient and colorful. As it stands, it is untranslatable into Western terms. However, great Indian masters — who have themselves studied the tradition and worked extensively with these subtle energies in their own bodies — have introduced these ideas to the West in ways that we can easily understand and work with.

INTERPENETRATING SHEATHS OR BODIES

The most obvious sheath is the physical body, because its slow vibratory level makes it visible to the naked eye — which is designed to see that particular range. Animals have different types of eyesight, that respond to different levels of vibration.

Less dense, interpenetrating the physical human body and slightly overlapping it, is the energy body. Kirlian photography reveals it as a pattern of light extending beyond, say, the visible hand. Kirlian photography also picks up the energy bodies of plants, showing how quickly the energy disappears and "dies" once the plant has been cut.

Our next body is the mental body, vibrating at a much higher level than the previous two, interpenetrating them and extending far beyond them. We can feel a change of atmosphere as soon as an angry or disturbed person walks into the room. The activities of the autonomic nervous system affect this body, which can feel very uncomfortable when it is in an ongoing state of imbalance or nervous tension.

Besides registering emotion, this mental body is like a computer, taking care of our everyday thinking. Much of what goes on in our heads is simply a continuous re-run of the programs that we have, over the years, fed into our "personal computer." This is why it is so hard to change our habits and attitudes — we have to go to a higher authority, at a higher level of vibration, to get the programs rewritten.

This higher authority is our higher mind, which interpenetrates the other bodies and extends beyond them. This body has many names — it is called conscience, and is the body of inner knowledge, of experience, of wisdom and discrimination. It is the body of informed and impartial choice, in contrast to the lower mental body which does our everyday reacting and thinking without much awareness, concerned only and always with the interests of Number One.

There is one more body, the finest of all, which extends beyond time and space. This is our soul body, which is sometimes called "the sheath of bliss" or "the gossamer raiment," because it lies next to the spirit and travels with it from before birth, through earthly life and beyond death into the worlds beyond.

Our birth is but a sleep and a forgetting:
The Soul that rises with us, our life's Star,
Hath had elsewhere its setting,
And cometh from afar.[1]

All five of these bodies are natural things. Even the soul, or causal body, has a material aspect which is shed at death, so that the spiritual essence can move into the timeless realm of spirit or pure consciousness. All of these bodies are subject to change, which is the underlying quality of all nature (see Chapter 4, page 19) — matter, energy and mind are one. They are nature in different forms. As Sir Arthur Eddington said: "The stuff of the world is mind stuff."

Healing with meditation deals with nature as "mind stuff," bringing the physical body, the energy body, the lower and higher mental bodies, and the soul body, into harmony with each other.

How can we think of the soul as nature? The fundamental quality of nature is change; the fundamental quality of spirit is that it is unchanging. If the soul were to leave this earth at death unchanged from when it arrived here at birth, what would be the point of incarnating at all? It changes through the experience it gains on earth. Patanjali — together with today's Hindus and Buddhists — took it for granted that we all incarnate many times before we finally become enlightened.

Why does spirit, wrapped in the gossamer raiment of a soul, and protected by layers of coarser bodies, choose to incarnate? Patanjali has a sublime answer: "It is only for the sake of the (Supreme) Self that the world exists . . . The Self is obscured by the world (of nature) in order that the reality of both may be discovered. Ignorance is destroyed by the undisturbed discrimination between the Self and the world."[2]

The world of nature changes constantly, moving through time and space, appearing as matter or energy or mind. Spirit (the self, or pure consciousness) is unchanging. We are destined to discover, and to experience, change and changelessness — and to recognize the difference between them.

THE CHAKRAS

Our five bodies of varying densities are joined together in many places by energy centers called chakras. The chief line of chakras lies along the spine. They are like transformers, which draw in energies and transform them to the right "frequency" for the job to be done. The main chakras have very specific jobs to do, involving all five bodies in the various processes. It is helpful to describe the main jobs of the chakras under the three groupings of life, love and light, before going into more detail.

Awareness of the chakras can be developed through visualization, chanting and getting in touch with the sensations in the body. All these methods will be more successful if you are already in the state of meditation before starting, rather than just thinking about chakras. Familiarity with these energies helps us to get them into better balance, harmonizing all the different aspects of nature within us.

There are three main chakras below the waist, situated at three points along the lower spine. These points open out into funnels of energy, which can be felt in the abdominal area. The energy here is life energy, concerned with the survival and health of the species (security), social interaction and self-esteem. These energies are necessary, amoral and totally self-centered. They form the foundation upon which all higher activities, feelings and thoughts depend.

There are two chakras along the upper spine, connected with breathing and the chest. The energy here is love energy, concerned with relationships and communication. This energy extends beyond the individual, involving him or her in concern for others and the good of all, in responsibility for others, in nurturing and caring and the expression of love.

There are two chakras in the head. The energy here is light energy, concerned with the mind, ideals, the soul's purpose for this particular life and its eternal connection with universal spirit or consciousness.

CHANTING OM OR AUM

Energy, like electricity, is felt as movement, warmth and illumination. We can feel these differences by breathing or chanting into the body's natural cavities, the abdominal, thoracic and skull spaces.

Sit in your meditation posture, and become aware of the floor of the body, the perineum. Pull up and tighten this pelvic floor, so that it feels as tight as a drum. This is the base of the abdominal area. The top of this abdominal space is the diaphragm muscle, which stretches across the whole body and separates the abdomen from the chest.

Keep your awareness in the abdominal space, and breathe in deeply, taking your hands and arms up overhead. As you breathe out, chant "Aaah," exploding this sound into the abdominal space and pushing the hands firmly down to abdominal level to help bring the sound down. Feel it bouncing off the perineum and the lower side of the diaphragm, reverberating through the abdominal cavity. Repeat this several times. The tone will be naturally low-pitched, as it sounds through the life centers — security, social interaction and self-esteem.

Move your attention to the chest space, bounded by the diaphragm muscle at the base and the vocal chords at the top. Breathe in deeply, and take the hands and arms up overhead. As you breathe out, chant "Oooh" into the chest space, bringing the hands down to heart level. Feel the sound reverberating in and warming the chest area. Repeat this several times. The tone will be naturally higher-pitched and sweet, as it sounds through the love centers — relationship and communication.

Move your attention to the skull space, bounded by the vocal chords at the base and the fontanelle at the top. The fontanelle is soft in babies, with the skin stretched tightly across it. Imagine that you have a soft fontanelle that can vibrate to sound. Breathe in deeply, taking your hands and arms up overhead. As you breathe out, chant "Mmm" into the skull space, bringing the hands down to eye level. Feel the tone reverberating in the skull as light clearing the mind of darkness and confusion. Repeat this several times. The tone will be naturally high and clear, as it sounds through the light centers — mind and spirit.

Now, with your hands quiet in your lap or on your thighs, chant "Aaah, Ooh, Mmm" feeling the sound in the body as before. Carry on in your own time and on your own natural note for as long as you wish. Then listen to the silence — the most important note of all.

The same exercise can be done mentally, lying down. It brings awareness of the different energies in the chakras. (For more about OM, see Chapter 13, page 99.)

USING COLOR

To enhance the sensitivity gained through using sound, you can use color in the same way. Breathe different colors out into each cavity. Use warm colors for the abdominal centers (red, orange, gold, yellow); peaceful colors for the thoracic centers (green, pink, turquoise, blue); and ethereal colors for the skull centers (midnight blue, deep purple, dove grey, lilac, shimmering white).

Life = Sat, Light = Chit, Love = Ananda. Together the centers add up to Satchitananda, which is the Sanskrit name for spirit as a Trinity. With a little study of the traditional correspondences, it is easy to create visualizations and meditations that stimulate the chakras in each of the three cavities.

When working on your own, do be sure that you balance these energies. We are apt to be attracted to practices that are easy for us because they work on centers that are already "awake" if not over-active. We should persevere with those that are not so rewarding, to sensitize and awaken under-active energies. Remember that all is nature, in different forms. No one form is better or worse than another. We need them all, from self-preservation at the base of the spine to connection with spirit at the crown of the head.

This is why a good teacher is advisable, to point out what we are hiding from ourselves. As a general rule, when working with the chakras, start with light to wake up the mind. Then go to life to energize the body and increase the ability to deal successfully with life's challenges, as an individual. Then work with love to dispel fear, open the heart and be in communion with a wider world than the individual self. End by integrating all the centers with breathing or chanting, or visualizations of colors or symbols for all the chakras.

CLOSING DOWN

Be absolutely sure to bring the energies back to base, and to use a strong grounding technique before coming out of meditation. Here are some suggestions.

"Draw," in your mind, a cross in a circle over each chakra, in either silver or gold. Start with the crown, close it with the cross and circle, and repeat at the brow. Continue down to the base, closing each chakra in turn. Then breathe strongly and deeply. Then become aware of your body, before moving your fingers, toes and neck. Be totally *in* your body before opening your eyes. You will notice that you come *out* of meditation by moving from the subtle to the gross sheaths — just as you move from the physical body to the energy body and then the mental body as you go *in* to meditation.

Another technique is to chant OM into each chakra, from the crown downward, to close them. Or you can see them as "flowers" that are bright and open when you are meditating. When you are ready to come out of meditation, you can gently "stroke" each one with an imaginary finger, so that the petals close over the brightness concealed within. Again, start at the crown and work down to the base.

It is as inappropriate to walk around with your chakras open as it is to go out of your home unprotected from the elements. You may like to throw an imaginary cloak around yourself before going into noisy public places. As you become sensitive to subtle energies, so you will come to feel the need to respect them.

SOME CHAKRA ASSOCIATIONS

Life chakras in the abdominal cavity:

- *Base:* This center is at the very base of the spine, so that you "sit on it." The color is red, the element is earth, the sense is smell. It is concerned with procreation, species survival, personal survival and security. The lower limbs (the legs and feet) are extensions of this chakra.

- *Sacral:* This center is located in the lower abdomen. The color is orange, the element is water, the sense is taste. It is concerned with social interaction, role-playing, pleasure, sensuality.

- *Navel:* This center is in the upper abdomen. The color is gold or yellow, the element is fire, the sense is sight. It is concerned with personal ambition, success and self-esteem.

Love chakras in the chest cavity:

- *Heart:* This center is in the middle of the chest. The color is green, the element is air, the sense is touch. It is concerned with relationship at a caring level, nurturing and being nurtured, reaching out to others. The upper limbs (the hands and arms) are extensions of this chakra.

- *Throat:* This center lies where the chest meets the neck. The color is blue, the element is sound, the sense is hearing. It is concerned with speech, communication, responsibility, creative expression.

Light chakras in the skull cavity:

- *Brow:* This center is in the middle of the head, with its third eye in the center of the forehead. The color is purple, indigo, midnight blue or smoky grey. The element is mind-intellect, intuition and insight.

- *Crown:* This center is at the crown, some say above it. The color is white or iridescent. The element is spirit — therefore some claim that it cannot be a chakra at all. Certainly it connects us with all that is beyond time and space and the phenomenal world.

Although the chakra system is not common knowledge in the West, it has always been known and used by healers. Many systems of psychotherapy and self-transformation use this knowledge in their visualizations.

---

[1] "William Wordsworth, "Intimations of Immortality," *The Oxford Dictionary of Quotations*, 2nd Edition, Oxford University Press 1954, p. 576.

[2] "Alistair Shearer, *Effortless Being*, London: Wildwood House 1982, Chapter 2, v. 21–6.

13

EASTERN MANTRAS

BALANCING OUR MATERIAL AND SPIRITUAL POLES

We may want to center ourselves more deeply in our own religious tradition, or in spirituality generally, because we feel that the material aspect of life dominates the spiritual to an unhealthy degree. We may even feel convinced that we *must* find a balance between these complementary opposites, and will remain "stuck" until we do so.

The practice of repeating a mantra during meditation, after settling ourselves with posture and breathing, is the quickest and most effective way of taking ourselves into a spiritual dimension. There are mantras for everyone, of every religious persuasion — Christian mantras for Christians, Buddhist mantras for Buddhists, Hindu mantras for Hindus, and some that are universal.

We may be looking for a spiritual dimension outside our own culture. We may believe that the

Eastern traditions of Hinduism and Buddhism have more to offer than the kind of Christianity we have been exposed to. Very often, the way forward seems to involve stepping sideway to get around obstacles that block our path. We may come back to our own tradition in the end, enriched by a wider view. Or we may settle happily into another tradition. The important thing is to make the connection with the spiritual pole of our being.

TRANSCENDENTAL MEDITATION (TM)

Millions of people in the West have turned to transcendental meditation for help, and their lives have been transformed. Swami Satyananda says:

It was in the mid-1960s that Maharashi Mahesh Yogi became well known in the United States. He chose an ideal time to introduce his system of "transcendental meditation." His name and techniques were fairly well established when masses of alienated young people were turning away from drugs and were seeking a surer path to greater awareness and spiritual insight. . . . Maharashi presented a simple and practical method of attaining peace and relaxation which was readily accepted by all aspirants regardless of their age, religion, intellectual ability and cultural background. Such a system was just what the west was greatly in need of. Today (1980) in Canada and America there are over 600,000 practitioners, with 10,000 more every month . . . and in Europe, the UK, India, Australia and New Zealand the number is also increasing.[1]

This technique involves simply sitting for meditation and repeating the mantra that has been chosen for you personally, according to criteria that are never divulged. Nor is the meaning of the mantra itself made known. Mantra is always concerned with an aspect of divinity, so you must just trust that fact, and use it daily. Others will have been given the same mantra, but that does not matter — the relationship between the mantra and its user is personal and unique. Its power builds up the more the mantra is repeated.

Transcendental meditation was brought to the West from India, and is rooted in the Hindu tradition. The divine energies associated with Hindu mantras naturally belong to Hindu deities, which are all symbols of energies already present in the universe and in human beings. Christians, or other followers of a particular religion, may not feel comfortable repeating sounds associated with Hindu deities, in which case they need to choose a mantra from their own religious tradition (see Chapter 14, "Christian Meditation Techniques," page 107).

Transcendental meditation is not suitable for anyone who feels a conflict between a Hindu mantra and their own religion. The Hindu religion itself, however, teaches that there is no such conflict. In it, all faiths are respected, being seen as different paths up the same mountain, and their founders as inspired by the same "One without a second." So, if you are searching for a way to counteract the materialism of Western society and have not found it in your own church, then TM or some other type of Eastern mantra meditation may be just what you need to start you on your spiritual journey.

Looking Both Ways

Let us look again at Mother Julian of Norwich. Anne Bancroft, in *The Luminous Vision,* says of her:

Her remarkable and mysterious revelations were equalled by her thoughtful, contemplative understanding of them . . . She was an anchoress — a hermit living in a cell built onto a church in Norwich . . . Her cell would have had at least two windows. One of these opened onto the church, so that she could take part in all services; and the other opened onto the outside world. People who wanted advice or consolation would come to this outside window and thus she kept in touch with the life of the town. When she was in meditation and not to be disturbed, a curtain embroidered with a cross would be drawn over the window. That she had plenty of visitors is not to be doubted. Norwich was second in size only to London at that time.[2]

Surely what we all need is to have two windows. Then we can alternate between the spiritual and the material aspects of life, and keep them in balance. Meditation can — and will if we permit it — open both these windows wider.

What we *do* (Patanjali's self-discipline), what we *know* (through the study of ourselves and of the sacred scriptures of the world) and what we *feel* (through self-surrender to that which we worship and long for most of all) can all be increased by keeping the activities outside our two windows in balance — and closing the curtains for meditation at regular intervals.

MANTRA GIVEN BY A GURU

In the Hindu tradition, if you want to use mantra, you will ask your guru to give you one. The guru is a spiritual preceptor, a teacher or guide in spiritual matters, who belongs to a long lineage of gurus. They will all have been trained in a tradition where mantra is the natural tool to use for spiritual advancement. Transcendental meditation follows this tradition, as do many traditions associated with Yoga.

THE UNIVERSAL MANTRA

This is the sound of OM or AUM. Here is what Patanjali says about it:

The deeper state of meditation . . . can also come from complete surrender to the almighty Lord. The Lord is a unique being, who exists beyond all suffering. . . . In Him lies the finest seed of all knowledge. Being beyond Time, He is the Teacher of even the most ancient tradition of teachers. He is expressed through the sound of the sacred syllable OM.[3]

To help us to get a fuller picture of this Lord, to whom the sound of OM refers, and to whom we should completely surrender ourselves, we can turn to one of the oldest sacred texts of India. In it we first of all find a description of the spiritual dimension:

That is full, this is full. From full the full is taken; the full has come. If you take out full from the full, the full alone remains.[4]

What a wonderful vision of all-ness, one-ness, complete-ness, ever-flowing sufficiency and abundance this is! What a contrast with the experience of not enough to go round, and having to grab your share, that characterizes the material world that we so often feel ourselves trapped in! Who dwells in this universe? Who rules or governs it?

"All this, whatsoever moves in this universe, is indwelled by the Lord."[5]

Swami Satyananda, in his commentary on this verse, writes:

The word used here for "Lord" or "God" is derived from a root word which means "to rule, to govern or to conduct." Therefore the "Lord" may be known as the Supreme Lord, or the Supreme Governor, or the Supreme Ruler. (This) should be understood as an all-pervading and all-governing essence. There is one unifying and permeating and underlying essence as a common link. It is not different in you and me. There is oneness of reality.[6]

Satya Sai Baba says: "(This) Name means the Lord of all Living Beings."[7] This, then, is the Lord, the Name, that is expressed by the mantra OM. This is also why OM is a universal mantra that anyone may use. How should we use it? Patanjali tells us: "OM should be repeated and its essence realized."[8]

REPETITION OF THE MANTRA

When you are settled and your breath is flowing smoothly, let the mantra OM start to float in and out with your breath.

(See the instructions for the mantra SO HAM at the end of Chapter 8, pages 59–60.)

You may like to lengthen your outbreath by silently saying one OM to each heartbeat. This comes quite naturally when you are relaxed. Somehow you know your own rhythm. If you are not sure, you can check against the artery in your wrist, or the carotid artery in your neck — there is one on each side of your Adam's apple. Once you have established the rhythm, you can repeat a few more OMs on the breath out than on the breath in, to make the outbreath longer.

Another method is to breathe in naturally and chant OM out loud as you breathe out, making the sound as smooth and long as possible. The OM should be all on the same note, as deep as your voice can comfortably manage. This allows for overtones in higher octaves. This low sound resonating in the silence around you is accompanied by higher vibrations, which you may be able to hear.

Chant for as long as your stillness and concentration hold, then stop and listen to the silence, which is now so full. The silence is as important as the sound.

Let the world impinge again on your consciousness very slowly. Take a few deep breaths and stretch your body before you get up from your meditation position. Mantra is heady stuff. Many meditators feel the need to bring the head to the floor before getting up, in order to ground their energies. If you are sitting in a chair, do be sure to feel your feet pressing firmly against the floor, and ground yourself that way before you stand up.

OM can also be chanted as AUM, pronounced "Aah . . . ooh . . . mmm." This is particularly good with a group, as the different sounds blend together. It is also good to chant in harmony rather than in unison, so that instead of all starting and finishing together, each person starts and finishes in his or her own time. The leader — if there is one — stops when it seems appropriate to do so, and the followers gradually fall silent in their own time. After a period of silence, the leader may decide to begin again.

KNOWING WHAT DIFFERENT MANTRAS MEAN

Do we need to know what a mantra means before we start to use it? Some teachers say that we should not concern ourselves about the meaning of the mantra, because this is fed to us at an unconscious level as we continue faithfully to repeat it during our meditation practice. Certainly there is a lot of truth in this — mantra does seem to have a slow release mechanism, which reveals the meaning slowly over time. We cannot begin to appreciate the whole depth of any mantra by examining it intellectually. It has to be lived until it becomes so much a part of us that we know it from the inside.

On the other hand, because we in the West rely so much upon the intellect, and may not belong to an ancient tradition which reveres its teachers without question, we may need to know what we are saying before we can let go into it. It may be best for us to choose our own mantra — preferably one that has been used by many others before us.

Rupert Sheldrake explains why:

Remember that morphic resonance enables people to connect with what's happened before; it can lead to a kind of collapse of time. So, the use of a mantra or ritual would enable someone doing it now to connect with those who have done it before. Now, if those who've done it before have attained an expansive or unitive consciousness through this mantra, then chanting it would serve to tune the practitioner in to that state. So, according to morphic resonance, it's not the mantra itself that leads to the visionary or transformative experience; it's the fact that the mantra connects or tunes into other people who've used the same practice to attain higher consciousness. . . .[9]

So, if you wish to benefit from the practice of mantra, begin by choosing a mantra that has already been empowered by a long tradition, rather than making up one of your own.

TRADITIONAL HINDU MANTRAS

Here are some short Hindu mantras, together with some suggestions as to their meaning.

OM NAMAH SHIVAYA. Shiva is pure consciousness, understood as male, passive, all-seeing and all-knowing. He is the complementary opposite of Shakti, understood as the female, active energy of nature. In most of our lives there is too much activity and not enough clarity, so we repeat the name of pure consciousness to redress our imbalance in this respect.

HARE KRISHNA, HARE KRISHNA. KRISHNA, KRISH-NA, HARE, HARE. HARE RAMA, HARE RAMA. RAMA, RAMA, HARE, HARE. This is known as the great mantra, and is used by the Krishna consciousness movement all over the world. Krishna is an *avatar* (incarnation or manifestation of a deity in human form), and Rama is the perfect man.

Krishna said of himself:

I have had many births, and so have you — but I remember all of mine, and you remember none of yours. In my ultimate self, though, I am changeless and am never ever born at all. I am the lord of all beings, and through my power of maya (illusion, as in glamour), I blend with nature and take shape . . . I reappear from age to age, for the protection of the good and the destruction of evil-doers.[10]

Krishna is thought of as the Lord of love, so this mantra is chanted to open our hearts to love.

SHRI RAM JAYA RAM. This mantra refers to Rama, a great king who was also the perfect man, always in tune with the divine will. His exploits are told in a vast epic of colorful stories, much loved by Hindus of all ages. Connection to a perfect human being may, by morphic resonance, help us to overcome our faults — especially our self-will.

RADHA, RADHA, RADHA GOVINDA, JAI! Paramahansa Yogananda has translated this mantra as "Spirit and nature dancing together. Victory to spirit! Victory to nature!" He explains its meaning thus:

Govinda is one of the names of God often assigned to Lord Krishna, a divine incarnation; Radha is the name of Krishna's greatest woman devotee. Their spiritual oneness symbolizes the inseparability of Spirit and its Shakti (creative power) or Nature. JAI means "hail!"[11]

Tapes of these and many other chants are available from specialized bookshops. You need gradually to absorb the pronunciation and rhythm by singing along with them, and playing them as background music around the house. The same applies to sacred chants from the other great traditions.

Note: Do not play mantra or relaxation tapes in the car, as they can make you feel either spaced out or drowsy.

TRADITIONAL BUDDHIST MANTRAS

These are often chanted by large assemblies of monks, on the lowest possible note. Tapes of these groups are awe-inspiring. So is the real thing, if you can join a Buddhist chanting session. Visitors are welcome at some Buddhist monasteries and centers.

OM MANI PADME HUM. This is often translated as "OM, the jewel in the lotus." The lotus plant is used as a symbol of purity. The lotus has its roots in the mud. It is firmly grounded in, and draws its sustenance from, nature — with all its chaotic energy, darkness and confusion. Its stalk passes up through the water, which represents the world of the emotions. Its leaves rise up out of the water and rest upon its surface, dry in the sun. So can we be in the world but not of it, refusing to allow the pull of the pairs of opposites to affect our equanimity. Finally, the flower opens its face to the sun, which represents the light of pure consciousness. The lotus plant, therefore, represents the evolved human being who, while remaining a part of nature, yet rises to become enlightened.

OM AH HUM, VAJRA GURU PADMA SIDDHI HUM. Vajra is strength that is as hard and bright as a diamond, impossible to bend or break. Guru is the spiritual preceptor who is the dispeller of darkness and who points the way we should go. The guru says: "Do not look at me. Look at where my finger points." Padma is the lotus plant. Siddhi is power, developed from spiritual practices, but never to be worshipped for its own sake. It is said of such power, if it is allowed to distract us from our path: "He who stops by the roadside to sell his wares will never complete his journey." So, strength and power are there to be gained, but are to be used only as the guru uses them — to show the way to others — and never for personal aggrandizement.

GATAY, GATAY, PARAGATAY. PARASAMGATAY, BODHI SVAHA! This is the mantra in Chapter Ten, which means "Beyond, beyond . . . beyond the Great Beyond. . . . Beyond even the thought of beyond . . . Homage to Thee."

The Christian approach to mantra practice is the subject of the next chapter.

---

[1] Swami Satyananda Saraswati, *Sure Ways to Self-Realisation,* Munger, India: Bihar School of Yoga 1980.

[2] Anne Bancroft, *The Luminous Vision — Six Medieval Mystics and Their Teachings,* London: Mandala 1989.

[3] Alistair Shearer, *Effortless Being,* London: Wildwood House 1982, Chapter 1, v. 23–7.

[4] Shanti Mantra, at the beginning of the *Ishavasya Upanishad*.

[5] Ibid., v. 1.

[6] Swami Satyananda Saraswati, *Commentary on the Ishavasya Upanishad*, Munger, India: Bihar School of Yoga 1973, p. 14.

[7] Quoted in *The Jesus Mystery*, Janet Bock, Los Angeles: Aura Books 1980.

[8] Alistair Shearer, *Effortless Being*, London: Wildwood House 1982, Chapter 1, v. 28.

[9] Rupert Sheldrake, speaking to Dan Menkin in *Quest* magazine, Theosophical Society Autumn 1995.

[10] Tom McArthur, *Yoga and the Bhagavad-Gita*, London: Aquarian Press 1986.

[11] Paramahansa Yogananda, *Cosmic Chants*, Los Angeles USA: Self-Realisation Fellowship 1974.

14

CHRISTIAN
MEDITATION
TECHNIQUES

MANTRA, PRAYER AND AFFIRMATION

Because Christianity presents God as three per-
sons, rather than as ultimate reality, the Christian
approach to God tends to be to tell Him your
troubles and to ask for His help. This is prayer
rather than mantra — although they can and do
overlap. Prayer, in this sense, is recognizing that
you need help in order to change things, and
therefore beseeching a divine person to intervene
in your life.

Affirmation, on the other hand, is pulling yourself together, and helping yourself by replacing a
negative outlook with a positive one. Affirmations are sentences or phrases which state in
the present tense those qualities we do not now
have, but hope to acquire in the future. Louise
Hay has written several excellent books which
use affirmations (see "Recommended Reading,"
page 120).

Care needs to be taken with this approach, as it implies a need for "more" of something that we presently lack — and this can knock us off our tightrope unless we are very firmly centered. Unfortunately, people are apt to be too hasty when it comes to getting rid of undesirable qualities and circumstances in their lives. This haste puts them back into stress mode and anxiety, and is therefore counter-productive. Patanjali is wise to insist upon self-knowledge.

Here is an example of the difference between prayer and affirmation — the subject is forgiveness. The prayer is: "Lord, how often the hurts that I've sustained in life have grieved me." (Talking to God, as *the* person who always understands.) "Strengthen my power of love, that I surrender all things to Thee, my eternal Friend." (Petition, asking God for help.) The affirmation given is: "All that befalls me is for my own good. I welcome any hurts that I receive as opportunities to grow in understanding."[1]

A resolve is also an affirmation, but is presented as a feeling or a becoming that is happening in the ever-present now. For instance: "From this moment on I am feeling more loving and understanding toward those who hurt me and (am) indifferent to the hurt." Whatever form is used, affirmations or resolves must be very carefully worded, to exclude anything negative. The unconscious mind does not understand the concept of "not." For example, "Whatever you do, never *think* of blue monkeys." You have to think of a blue monkey in order to then *not* think of it. Avoid negative words and concepts, too.

It can be seen from this description that both prayer and affirmation involve us in recognizing that something is amiss, and then doing something about it. Mantra, on the other hand, starts changes in us without any need for us first to consider what may be wrong in our personal circumstances or attitudes. By simply sitting quietly, letting go of all anxiety, settling the mind and repeating the mantra, we allow something to happen in us. Mantra practice raises our vibrations, so that we are more in touch with the divine within, more ready to see things differently, and to change our attitudes accordingly. This contact with divine energies, through raising our own vibratory level, puts us in a better frame of mind. It brings release, healing and new strength. We can now pray more deeply and sincerely, or use affirmations more effectively.

In modern Western society, as discussed in Chapter 6, the pressure to be always actively busy makes our nervous systems very unbalanced. We urgently need regular periods where we stop "doing" and start "being." As we know, this balance can be achieved through the regular practice of meditation.

Throughout the history of Christianity, there has always been one group of people who have been encouraged to keep this balance — those who have lived in seclusion in monasteries and convents. Their days are lived to a rhythm where activity alternates with periods of silence, chanting, private prayer and meditation.

Well-meaning Christian lay people, on the other hand, often feel that more and more "doing" is being asked of them. Yet we could all give so much more — and give it so much more willingly — if we first learned to balance our nervous systems, clear our minds and open our hearts through the regular practice of meditation. This is at last being realized, however, and there have been significant movements in recent years to make Christian meditation meaningful and available to all. Examples of Christian mantra follow.

Wherever there is praise *to* God, rather than a request *for* something, there is mantra. There is upliftment and a tuning in to higher levels. An example is "The Lord's Prayer," which starts and ends with a string of mantras where the focus is always on God, thereby lifting us up and out of ourselves.

"Our Father" is a mantra that links us to an aspect of divinity, the fatherhood of the God who created us, cares for us and lovingly arranges for our education in the school of life to match our needs and abilities as we develop. This Father is also a Daddy, who listens to His little children with respect and affection. Jesus said:

Would any of you who are fathers give your son a stone, when he asks you for bread? Or would you give him a snake, when he asks you for fish? As bad as you are, you know how to give good things to your children. How much more, then, your Father in heaven will give good things to those who ask him.[2]

Perhaps, if we have had bad experiences from our fathers, or as fathers ourselves, we also need to affirm this mantra — to put Jesus' idea of what it means to be God the Father in the place of our own negative attitudes toward fatherhood. What better time could there be for such an affirmation to take root than when we are in a deep and reverent state of meditation?

"Who art in Heaven" is another statement about divinity rather than about ourselves. We know that Heaven lies within us, therefore God does too. "Hallowed be Thy Name!" is the essence and purpose of mantra, to raise ourselves to a level of vibration that desires only to praise what is holy. "Thy kingdom come" is mantra, because it is about God and His plan. It is also petition, because it is what we want, too. It is also affirmation, because it replaces our negative fears about the future and the present dire state of the world.

"Thy will be done!" is also mantra, because it is about God. Even if we are unwilling either to pray for this outcome or to affirm it, the regular use of this mantra will soften our self-will and help us with Patanjali's "essential preliminary attitude" of self-surrender.

Almost every word of "The Lord's Prayer" can be understood and used as mantra *before* thinking of it as prayer or
affirmation. We praise God for what and how He is. Only
later do we consider how this may affect us, and our own
lives and attitudes.

The Taizé Experience

Brother Roger, of Taizé in France, has spent many years
putting Christian prayers and sacred phrases to simple
music that can be chanted. A few words — or one word,
such as Alleluia! — are chanted over and over again. The
very simple tune is set in four parts, which can be quickly
learned by anyone. These four parts rise and fall in waves of
sacred sound — mantra. Latin, such as *Adoramus te Domine*,
is used — perhaps for its morphic resonance across the
Christian centuries — in addition to English, French, Ger-
man and other European languages.

Taizé music is being used more and more in churches. It is
so simple, devout and repetitive that it lifts you straight into
a deep state of meditation. Young people, who may not nor-
mally be churchgoers, flock to Taizé in their thousands
every summer, backpacking from all parts of Europe to
camp there.

The Taizé phenomenon shows what a spiritual thirst there is
in Europe for Christian meditation, brought about by sacred
music and chanting.

The Mantra Centers Started by Dom John Main

This is another worldwide movement started by one
inspired man, who was determined to bring meditation
with mantra to modern lay Christians. Dom John Main was
a Benedictine monk who died in 1982. St. Benedict inspired
the vast monastic movement that flowered in medieval
Europe, and he, in turn, was inspired by John Cassian.

Dom John Main writes:

Just as thousands of young people today make their pilgrimage to the east in search of wisdom and personal authority, so Cassian and his friend Germanus journeyed to the deserts of Egypt where the holiest and most famous men of the spirit were to be found in the fourth century . . . They asked Abbot Isaac the simple question: "How do we pray? Teach us, show us."

The answer, Cassian writes, is this: "The mind should unceasingly cling to the mantra until, strengthened by continual use of it, it casts off and rejects the rich and ample matter of all kinds of thought and restricts itself to the poverty of the single verse . . . Those who realize this poverty arrive with ready ease at the first of the beatitudes: Blessed are they who are poor in spirit for theirs is the Kingdom of Heaven."

The spiritual life for Cassian, the serious perseverance in the poverty of the single verse, is a Passover. By persevering, we pass from sorrow to joy, from loneliness to communion. We must know for ourselves in the depth of our own being. We must perform rather than teach, be rather than do . . . The simple practical means he teaches is the unceasing use of the mantra. We cannot achieve the Kingdom of God by our own efforts or think our way into it, and so we have a simpler more immediate goal which he calls "purity of heart." This is all we should concern ourselves with, he teaches. The rest will be given to us. And the way to purity of heart, to full and clear awareness, is the way of poverty, the "grand poverty" of the mantra.[3]

The mantra that Dom John Main has left with us, and which is used by all who practice in the centers that bear his name, is MARANATHA. He instructs:

Sit down. Sit still and upright. Close your eyes lightly. Sit relaxed but alert. Silently, interiorly, begin to say a single word. We recommend the prayer-phrase "maranatha." Recite it as four sylla-

bles of equal length. Listen to it as you say it, gently but continuously. Do not think or imagine anything — spiritual or otherwise. If thoughts and images come, these are distractions at the time of meditation, so keep returning to simply saying the word. Meditate each morning and evening for between twenty and thirty minutes.[4]

Dom John Main explains why he has chosen this word MARANATHA:

There are various mantras which are possible for a beginner. If you have no teacher to help you, then you should choose a word that has been hallowed over the centuries by our Christian tradition. Some of these words were first taken over as mantras for Christian meditation by the Church in its earliest days. One of these is the word "maranatha." It is the Aramaic word which means, "Come Lord. Come Lord Jesus." It is the word that St. Paul uses to end his first letter to the Corinthians, and the word with which St. John ends the book of Revelation. I prefer the Aramaic form, because it has no associations for most of us and it helps us into a meditation that will be quite free of all images.

Keep to the word you choose. If you chop and change your mantra you are postponing your progress in meditation.[5]

"THE CLOUD OF UNKNOWING"

Dom John Main writes: "A thousand years after Cassian, the English author of *The Cloud of Unknowing* recommends the repetition of a little word: 'We must pray in the height, depth, length, and breadth of our spirit, not in many words but in a little word.' "[6]

The author of *The Cloud of Unknowing* is unknown, except that he was an English priest writing to a student — a young man of twenty-four — in the fourteenth century. He was greatly influenced by Dionysius (sometimes called pseudo Dionysius, as this may have been a pen-name). The translation of Dionysius from Greek into Latin in the ninth century provided new inspiration from the Greek Orthodox tradition.

The Cloud of Unknowing is a treasure trove of teachings about the spiritual life. One excerpt, on mantra, will give the flavor of it:

So when you feel by the grace of God that he is calling you to this work (of contemplation or "meditation"), and you intend to respond, lift your heart to God with humble love. It all depends on your desire. A naked intention directed to God, and himself alone, is wholly sufficient.

If you want this intention summed up in a word, to retain it more easily, take a short word, preferably of one syllable, to do so. The shorter the word the better, being more like the working of the spirit. A word like God or Love. Choose which you like, or perhaps some other, so long as it is of one syllable. And fix this word fast to your heart, so that it is always there come what may. It will be your shield and spear in peace and war alike. With this word you will hammer the cloud (of unknowing) and the darkness above you. With this word you will suppress all thought under the cloud of forgetting.[7]

THE PATH AND THE GOAL

Let some mystics from various spiritual traditions conclude this chapter.

A Sufi (early twentieth century): "We cannot ask thee for aught, for thou knowest our needs before they are born in us: Thou art our need; and in giving us more of thyself thou givest us all."[8]

A Hindu (early twentieth century): "This is my prayer to thee, my Lord — strike, strike at the root of penury in my heart . . . Give me the strength to surrender my strength to thy will with love."[9]

A Moslem influenced by Sufism and Hinduism (fifteenth century): "It is time to put up a love-swing! Tie the body and then tie the mind so that they swing between the arms of the Secret One you love . . . listen to me, brother, bring the shape, face, and odour of the Holy One inside you."[10]

Christian (fourteenth century): "We have the power to ask of our Lover, reverently, all that we desire. For our natural desire is to have God and the good desire of God is to have us. We can never stop this desire or longing until we have our Lover in the fullness of joy. Then can we no more desire."[11]

Sufi (thirteenth century): "All medicines are just images of the loving of the lover, whose face looks inward, with no kin but the one You."[12]

[1] J. Donald Walters, *Affirmations and Prayers*, California: Crystal Clarity 1988, p. 29.

[2] St. Matthew, *Good News for Modern Man*, Chapter 7, v. 9.

[3] John Main, *Word into Silence*, London: Darton, Longman and Todd 1980, pp 61–4.

[4] Ibid., p. v.

[5] Ibid., p. 11.

[6] Ibid., p. 10.

[7] Clifton Wolters (tr.), *The Cloud of Unknowing*, London: Penguin Classics 1961, p. 69.

[8] Kahlil Gibran, *The Prophet*, London: Pan 1980, p. 82.

[9] Rabindranath Tagore, Song 36, *Gitanjali*, London: Macmillan.

[10] Robert Bly (tr.), *The Kabir Book*, Canada: Beacon Press 1977, p. 36.

[11] Brendan Doyle, *Julian of Norwich*, USA: Bear and Co. 1983, p. 31.

[12] Rumi, Coleman Barks (tr.), *One-Handed Basket Weaving*, USA: Maypop 1991.

15

GROUP MEDITATION

INVOLVING OTHERS

Meditating with other people can be a very powerful experience. The fact that it moves us so deeply may indicate that it is also effective as a tool for change in a wider arena than our personal selves. We may wish to change or heal the planet, or human attitudes toward the planet.

Meditating in a group has its own dynamic, and therefore its own rules. The first need is to bring the group together, so that it meditates as a unit. Just sitting together in a quiet space is not enough. In fact, this can be most unwise — unless the group has already been working together and become united. For the safety of all concerned, group meditation requires a preliminary purifying and harmonizing of individual energies and a responsible, watchful leader who does not get carried away.

For instance, it is very pleasant to have a natural meditation period at the end of a Yoga class. In this situation, we have a teacher who watches over us, decides when to bring the silence to a close and takes responsibility for our joint psychic well-being. The teacher must not meditate — to do so would be to turn inward, and to abandon the students who have entrusted themselves to him or her.

GROUP PURPOSE

It is a waste of our energies not to have a group purpose in coming together to meditate. It can also be very helpful, especially for beginners, to have a leader who talks the group through the meditation. It helps people to stay focused for longer periods if they can come back from their drifting to a voice reminding them of why they are there.

When we meditate as a group, we will naturally choose a topic of interest to the group, which should not be too parochial. Personal problems can be addressed in our private meditation time. However, some healing groups do focus on personal problems, using one member as the focus and asking for healing — that is, change — for that person. Again, do not be too specific. Healing comes in many unexpected forms — to demand from God some specific outcome is to deny, perhaps, far wider evidence of divine grace.

DEDICATION OF GROUP ENERGY

It is traditional to dedicate the efforts of the group, offering them in the service of the Most High. This neutralizes ego power building — particularly important for groups. Leader and members are merely instruments. "Leadership" is just an office that may pass in turn to any member willing to take it on. The energies released in the meditation provide fuel for change — and that is the only condition that can be set upon them. "Not my will, but Thy Will, be done."

It can be a good idea to put an object, such as a crystal or a flower, in the middle of the group to represent the Most High in our midst. Our eyes, even when closed, rest on this object — we thus focus all our energies on this point like a laser beam. Besides, still eyes create a still mind.

GROUP STRUCTURE

Groups need a structure, even more than individual meditations. One way to begin is to light a candle, representing our opening to the light. From this moment, all conversation ceases. The leader, topic and style will have already been decided. Any preliminary stretching or physical settling will have been completed. Nothing is to be put into this open space except what concerns the group as a whole, and the group purpose.

Ritualistic cleansing may follow — breathing, relaxing, opening the chakras, or whatever is appropriate — then the dedication. At some point, there may be prayers for named people — this should always come at the same point. The group should have a familiar routine and stick to it, so that everyone knows where they are. If anything new is to be tried, discuss it in detail before the candle is lit. The main meditation can last up to an hour for experienced meditators, perhaps ten minutes for beginners who find it more difficult to sit still.

CLOSING DOWN

It is extremely important to close down very thoroughly at the end of any meditation, particularly with a group. People in groups, especially if they meet regularly, become very open and trusting. They feel safe, among friends, with a responsible leader and in the presence of the divine. Life (pure energies), light and love mingle harmoniously. Unfortunately, the world outside this charmed circle is not so serene.

To retain this serenity deep within, it is necessary to protect ourselves. We use ritual — closing each chakra with a cross and circle, placing an invisible cloak around ourselves, earthing or grounding ourselves so that we are not left vulnerable and too heavenly to be any earthly use upon our return to the everyday world.

Giving Thanks

Finally, we give thanks for the opportunity to serve, for the strength and fellowship of the group and for the insight, grace and glory we may have personally experienced. We ask for grace to continue humbly working for the group cause. Then the candle is blown out, refreshments can be produced, and conversation resumes.

Group meditation is much needed to bond together people of goodwill, and to create that critical mass that changes the world.

RECOMMENDED READING

The Bible — Good News for Modern Man and Authorized Version.

The Yoga Sutras of Patanjali in four translations, with commentaries:

Prabhavananda, Swami and Isherwood, Christopher, *How to Know God,* London: Mentor, New English Library Limited 1969.

Satchidananda, Sri Swami, *Integral Yoga,* Virginia: Integral Yoga Publications 1978.

Shearer, Alistair, *Effortless Being,* London: Wildwood House 1982 (out of print).

Taimni, I. K., *The Science of Yoga,* London: Theosophical Publishing House 1961.

The teachings on meditation, subtle energies and chakras by Swami Satyananda Saraswati and his disciples, in numerous books. All published by the Bihar School of Yoga, Munger, India.

Bancroft, Anne, *The Luminous Vision — Six Medieval Mystics and Their Teachings*, London: Mandala 1989.

Disciples of Ajahn Chah, *Seeing the Way*, England: Amaravati Publications 1989.

Doyle, Brendan, *Meditations with Julian of Norwich*, New Mexico: Bear and Co. 1983.

Gawain, Shakti, *Creative Visualization*, USA: Bantam New Age Books 1978.

Hay, Louise L., *You Can Heal Your Life*, USA: Eden Grove Editions 1984.

Main, John, *Word into Silence*, London: Darton, Longman and Todd 1983.

Wolters, Clifton (tr.), *The Cloud of Unknowing*, London: Penguin Classics 1961.

INDEX

NOTES

NOTES

NOTES

NOTES

OTHER ULYSSES PRESS
HEALTH TITLES

ANXIETY AND DEPRESSION: A NATURAL APPROACH
Shirley Trickett

By addressing the patient's total health from a physical *and* mental standpoint, *Anxiety and Depression: A Natural Approach* avoids the failure of traditional medical treatment. With specific suggestions on diet, breathing, relaxation, bio-feedback, and exercise, the program helps sufferers empower themselves to prevent further discomfort. $8.95

THE BOOK OF KOMBUCHA
Beth Ann Petro

The Book of Kombucha explains the health benefits of the "tea mushroom" while answering the concerns surrounding this alternative health treatment. Draws on up-to-date research and explains how to grow and use Kombucha. $11.95

BREAKING THE AGE BARRIER:
STAYING YOUNG, HEALTHY AND VIBRANT
Helen Franks

Drawing on the latest medical research, *Breaking the Age Barrier* explains how the proper lifestyle can stop the aging process and make you feel youthful and vital. $12.95

COUNT OUT CHOLESTEROL
Art Ulene, M.D. and Val Ulene, M.D.

Complete with counter and detailed dietary plan, this companion resource to the *Count Out Cholesterol Cookbook* shows how to design a cholesterol-lowering program that's right for you. $12.95

COUNT OUT CHOLESTEROL COOKBOOK
Art Ulene, M.D. and Val Ulene, M.D.

A companion guide to *Count Out Cholesterol*, this book shows you how to bring your cholesterol levels down with the help of 250 gourmet recipes. $14.95

DISCOVER MEDITATION: A FIRST-STEP GUIDE TO BETTER HEALTH
Doriel Hall

> *Discover Meditation* leads the reader step by step through a journey of discovery into this ancient discipline. Chapters address everything from physical positioning and breathing techniques to focusing the mind and achieving self-knowledge. $8.95

DISCOVER OSTEOPATHY: A FIRST-STEP GUIDE TO BETTER HEALTH
Peta Sneddon and Paolo Coseschi

> In *Discover Osteopathy,* two practicing osteopaths explain simply and lucidly the basic principles of osteopathy, when to visit an osteopath, and how osteopathy works. Specific chapters detail osteopathic techniques, and special sections look at the application of these therapies in areas like pregnancy, childbirth, and even dentistry. $8.95

DISCOVER REFLEXOLOGY: A FIRST-STEP GUIDE TO BETTER HEALTH
Rosalind Oxenford

> *Discover Reflexology* relates this ancient tradition to its historical context within Chinese medicine and to the modern understanding of holistic health programs that address body, mind, and spirit. This book empowers the beginner to incorporate the therapy into his or her own personal program of good health. $8.95

DISCOVERY PLAY
Art Ulene, M.D. and Steven Shelov, M.D.

> This book guides parents through the first three years of their child's life, offering play activity with a special emphasis on nurturing self-esteem. $9.95

IRRITABLE BOWEL SYNDROME: A NATURAL APPROACH
Rosemary Nicol

> This book offers a natural approach to a problem millions of sufferers have. The author clearly defines the symptoms and offers a dietary and stress-reduction program for relieving the effects of this disease. $9.95

KNOW YOUR BODY: THE ATLAS OF ANATOMY
Introduction by Trevor Weston, M.D.

> Designed to provide a comprehensive and concise guide to the structure of the human body, *Know Your Body* offers more than 250 color illustrations. An easy-to-follow road map of the human body. $12.95

LAST WISHES: A HANDBOOK TO GUIDE YOUR SURVIVORS
Lucinda Page Knox, M.S.W. and Michael D. Knox, Ph.D.

A simple do-it-yourself workbook, *Last Wishes* helps people put their affairs in order and eases the burden on their survivors. It allows them to plan their own funeral and leave final instructions for survivors. $12.95

LOSE WEIGHT WITH DR. ART ULENE
Art Ulene, M.D.

This best-selling weight-loss book offers a 28-day program for taking off the pounds and keeping them off forever. $12.95

MOOD FOODS
William Vayda

Mood Foods shows how the foods you eat can influence your emotions, behavior, and personality. It also explains how a proper diet can help to alleviate such common complaints as PMS, hyperactivity, mood swings, and stress. $9.95

PANIC ATTACKS: A NATURAL APPROACH
Shirley Trickett

Addresses the problem of panic attacks using a holistic approach. Focusing on diet and relaxation, the book helps you prevent future attacks. $8.95

THE VITAMIN STRATEGY
Art Ulene, M.D. and Val Ulene, M.D.

A game plan for good health, this book helps readers design a vitamin and mineral program tailored to their individual needs. $11.95

YOUR NATURAL PREGNANCY:
A GUIDE TO COMPLEMENTARY THERAPIES
Anne Charlish

This timely book brings together the many complementary therapies such as aromatherapy, massage, homeopathy, acupressure, herbal medicine, and meditation, that can benefit pregnant women. $16.95

To order these or other Ulysses Press books call 800-377-2542 or write to Ulysses Press, P.O. Box 3440, Berkeley, CA 94703-3440. All retail orders are shipped free of charge. California residents must include sales tax. Allow two to three weeks for delivery.

Doriel Hall has taught and practised yoga and meditation from various traditions for many years, running a residential retreat center for this purpose. She is the author of *Starting Yoga*.